"Clear, wise, soulful, and poetic."
— ALANIS MORISSETTE

foreword by
ECKHART TOLLE

Parenting
with Presence

*Practices for Raising
Conscious, Confident,
Caring Kids*

SUSAN STIFFELMAN, MFT

Author of Parenting Without Power Struggles

• An Eckhart Tolle Edition •

Praise for *Parenting with Presence*

"This is exactly the advice and support you need as a parent! Seasoned, wise, and practical, *Parenting with Presence* helps parents take a deep breath and tend to themselves and their kids with compassion, love, and mindfulness."

— Jack Kornfield, author of *A Path with Heart*,
and Trudy Goodman, PhD, founder of InsightLA

"I've led a community of hundreds of thousands of parents for six years, and during that time I've recommended only one parenting book: *Parenting Without Power Struggles*. Now I finally have one more to insist they read: *Parenting with Presence*. I trust Susan Stiffelman with my heart, my family, and my community because she understands that parenting is not just a job but a spiritual practice — a path to healing, to truth, to God. She knows that what goes on in my home every day is brutal and beautiful and hard and holy. She understands that while we are raising our children, we are still raising ourselves. In *Parenting with Presence*, Susan comes alongside parents not only as an expert but as a guide, a counselor, a friend, a healer. This book will help adults heal so they can raise children who need a little less healing."

— Glennon Doyle Melton, author of the *New York Times* bestseller *Carry On, Warrior*, president of the nonprofit Together Rising, and founder of the online community at Momastery.com

"*Parenting with Presence* is a gentle but powerful reminder that our own awareness, our own calmness, and our ability to respond and not react to stressful situations are fundamental to raising healthy kids. It's more about us as parents than it is about them as children. And if we do the work on ourselves, then we can be circuit breakers for the flow of negative energy that escalates stressful situations. This is an important work."

— Tim Ryan, US Representative from Ohio
and author of *A Mindful Nation*

"With her clear, wise, soulful, and poetic writing, Susan Stiffelman shows us how both the blessings and challenges of the delicate child-parent relationship can be a hotbed for mutual growth, healing, and connection. With children determining the future of our planet, Susan lays the groundwork for us to usher this new generation toward a more healed, humane, and connected world, starting with our very own selves. I am so grateful to Susan for having written this powerful book."

— Alanis Morissette, singer/songwriter and activist

"Who knew that the child or teen crying in the next room is actually our spiritual teacher? Who would have thought that annoying outbursts and provocative behavior could lead to more conscious, spiritually tuned-in, effective, even enjoyable parenting? Susan Stiffelman's groundbreaking, immensely readable guide teaches all we need to know about how to nurture our children — and ourselves — to become more conscious, compassionate, and, believe it or not, calmer human beings."

— Kathy Eldon, founder and chairman
of the Creative Visions Foundation

"I stole it from my mother and devoured it! A fantastic read that should be mandatory for all parents. I cannot wait for it to come out so I can hand it out to everyone I know."

— Amy Eldon Turteltaub,
cofounder of the Creative Visions Foundation and
vice president of Creative Visions Productions

"An empathic tenderness runs through this wise and down-to-earth guide to parenting with greater awareness. You can feel the love that Susan Stiffelman has for the families she works with in her therapy practice and her confidence in all of us to grow into the challenges and gifts of being a parent. This book offers a beautiful, multifaceted articulation of what our children most need from us, and practices for both developing these competencies and drawing upon them for our children and for ourselves."

— Myla and Jon Kabat-Zinn, authors of
Everyday Blessings: The Inner Work of Mindful Parenting

"One of the best parenting books I've seen in a long while. With clarity, warmth, and wisdom, Susan Stiffelman bridges the world of spiritual transformation with the down-to-earth realities of parenting. *Parenting with Presence* is full of insights that will set parents on a path of healing and joy. I highly recommend it!"

— Elisha Goldstein, PhD, author of *Uncovering Happiness: Overcoming Depression with Mindfulness and Self-Compassion*

"As a mother, I found myself powerfully moved by the insights and exercises in *Parenting with Presence*. Susan Stiffelman delicately explores what many parenting experts avoid — the deeper layers of fear, guilt, and shame that thwart our ability to be fully present for those aspects of parenting we find most challenging. A beautiful offering to us all. I will forever be giving out this book as a gift to new and seasoned parents alike."

— Katherine Woodward Thomas, author of *Conscious Uncoupling*

"An enlightened guide to parenting for anyone wanting to raise caring, happy, resilient children while healing their own unfinished childhood issues, *Parenting with Presence* is filled with parental wisdom intelligently presented and richly woven with examples from real life. A gem of a book!"

— Marci Shimoff, author of *Happy for No Reason*

"*Parenting with Presence* is an invaluable guide for any parent wanting to raise children who understand what it truly means to live a successful life. With her mix of practical tools and personal stories, Susan Stiffelman shows how to create close, loving family relationships and captures just how transformational and fulfilling parenthood can be."

— Arianna Huffington, author of *Thrive*

"In *Parenting with Presence*, renowned expert Susan Stiffelman offers a unique way to bring up our children that combines both wisdom and compassion. Thoroughly practical, the approaches she shares in this remarkable book could help us parents create a strong basis for a truly loving and compassionate connection with our children, while also bringing out the best from us — our presence, joy, understanding, and kindness."

— Thupten Jinpa, principal English translator to the Dalai Lama and author of *A Fearless Heart*

"While reading *Parenting with Presence*, I kept saying to myself, 'I wish *my* parents had read this book!' Finally a book on parenting that speaks to *all* aspects of our 'inner child' and gives each of us the kind of guidance that not only educates but transforms, uplifts, and nurtures both child and parent. Bravo!"

— Janet Bray Attwood, *New York Times* bestselling author of *The Passion Test: The Effortless Path to Discovering Your Life Purpose*

"The core secret revealed in *Parenting with Presence* is that presence is the only effective way to interact with children. Presence includes support and structure — with that, children thrive; without that, children experience chaos, and parenting can be a nightmare. The second secret is that parenting is a growth process, and your child is your best teacher. Understanding both secrets prevents parenting that nurtures without structure and parenting that shapes without nurture. This book brings new awareness about a parenting process that increases the health of our culture itself. Recommended to all parents and parents-to-be."

— Harville Hendrix, PhD, and Helen LaKelly Hunt, PhD, authors of *Giving the Love That Heals: A Guide for Parents*

Parenting *with* Presence

*Practices for Raising Conscious,
Confident, Caring Kids*

SUSAN STIFFELMAN, MFT

Foreword by ECKHART TOLLE

• An Eckhart Tolle Edition •

New World Library
Novato, California

an
eckhart
tolle
edition

An Eckhart Tolle Edition
www.eckharttolle.com

New World Library
14 Pamaron Way
Novato, California 94949

Text design by Tona Pearce Myers

Library of Congress Cataloging-in-Publication Data is available.

First printing, April 2015
ISBN 978-1-60868-326-0
Printed in Canada on 100% postconsumer-waste recycled paper

New World Library is proud to be a Gold Certified Environmentally Responsible Publisher. Publisher certification awarded by Green Press Initiative. www.greenpressinitiative.org

10   9   8   7   6   5   4   3   2   1

To the children we are raising,
and the ones who live within our hearts,
may you discover that it is safe to come out to play,
to dance,
and to shine.

Contents

Foreword

To be allowed to drive a car, you need to pass both theoretical and practical tests so that you don't become a danger to yourself and others. For all except the most rudimentary jobs, certain qualifications are required, and for the more complex jobs, years of training. Yet for one of the most challenging and vitally important occupations — parenting — no training or qualifications are required.

"Parenthood remains the greatest single preserve of the amateur," wrote author Alvin Toffler. This lack of knowledge or education is one of the reasons (although not the main one, as we shall see) why so many parents struggle. Those parents don't necessarily fail to meet the child's physical and material needs. They may in fact love their child and want what is best for them. Yet they are clueless as to how to deal with the challenges their child presents them with on an almost daily basis, nor do they know how to respond appropriately to the growing child's emotional, psychological, and spiritual needs.

Whereas in past ages parenting was excessively authoritarian, in our contemporary society many parents fail to provide the clear guidance the child desperately needs and longs for. There is often a complete lack of structure in the home environment, which resembles a rudderless ship that has been abandoned by the captain, adrift in the ocean. The parents don't realize that the child needs them to be, as Susan Stiffelman so aptly calls it, "the Captain of the ship," a term that by no means implies reverting back to the authoritarian mode of education of past ages. Rather, it is about finding a balance, a middle way, between having an excess of structure and no structure at all.

Ultimately, though, the deeper cause of family dysfunction is not the parents' lack of knowledge or education but their lack of awareness. Without a conscious parent there can be no conscious parenting! A conscious parent is able to maintain a certain level of awareness in their daily life, even though for most people lapses are bound to happen from time to time. When there is no awareness (other names for it are *mindfulness* or *presence*), you relate to your child, as well as to everybody else, through the conditioning of your mind. You are in the grip of mental/emotional reactive patterns, beliefs, and unconscious assumptions that you absorbed from your parents and the surrounding culture you grew up in.

Many of these patterns go back countless generations into the distant past. However, when there is awareness — or presence, as I prefer to call it — you become aware of your own mental, emotional, and behavioral patterns. You begin to have a choice about how to respond to your children, rather than acting blindly out of old patterns. Also, most important, you no longer pass those patterns on to your children.

Without presence, you are only able to connect with the child through the thinking mind and emotions, rather than on the deeper level of Being. Even if you *do* all the right things, the most important ingredient in your relationship with your child will be missing: the Being dimension, which is the spiritual realm. This means the deeper connection just isn't there.

Intuitively, the child will sense that something vitally important in his or her relationship with you is missing, that you are never fully present, never fully there, always in your mind. Unconsciously, the child will then assume or rather feel that you are withholding something important. This frequently gives rise to unconscious anger or resentment in the child, which may manifest in various ways or remain latent until adolescence.

Although this alienation between parent and child is still the norm, a change is happening. An increasing number of parents are becoming conscious, able to transcend the conditioned patterns of their mind and connect with their child on the deeper level of Being.

So the reasons for dysfunctional or unconscious parenting are twofold. On the one hand, there is the lack of knowledge or education concerning child rearing that strikes a sane balance between the old, excessively authoritarian approach and the contemporary, equally unbalanced one. On the other hand, and at a more fundamental level, there is the lack of presence or conscious awareness on the part of the parents.

Whereas numerous books provide helpful "know-how" for those parents who read books, not many books as yet address the lack of awareness of the parents or offer guidance on how to use the everyday challenges of parenting as a way of growing in consciousness. Susan Stiffelman's book helps the reader on both levels, which we could call Doing and Being. She imparts insightful knowledge and practical advice on Doing (or Right Action, as the Buddhists call it), without neglecting the more fundamental level of Being.

Parenting with Presence shows parents how they can transform parenting into a spiritual practice. It helps turn the ways

your children challenge you into a mirror that allows you to become aware of your own hitherto unconscious patterns. And by
becoming aware of them, you can begin to transcend them.

Author Peter De Vries wrote: "Who of us is mature enough
for offspring before the offspring themselves arrive? The value
of marriage is not that adults produce children but that children
produce adults." Whether we are married or single parents, children will certainly help us grow into more mature human beings.
Yes, children produce adults, but, more important, Susan Stiffelman's unique book shows you how children can produce *conscious*
adults.

— Eckhart Tolle, author of
The Power of Now and *A New Earth*

Introduction

Angie was a powerhouse on the job. As the editor of a small health and wellness magazine, she got things done efficiently, thoroughly, and on time. Although her staff sometimes felt micromanaged, she went out of her way to create an appealing work environment, offering generous perks such as flexible telecommuting options and a break room stocked with organic snacks. But Angie was committed to leading a life that wasn't all about being productive. Every morning she listened to a guided meditation before getting ready for the day ahead, and before they had children, she and her husband, Eric, had made a point of going to yoga retreats whenever possible.

Eric had a small Internet marketing company based out of their home. He was known for his ability to think outside the box and enjoyed growing success based on his creativity and can-do, get-it-done-on-time reputation.

Angie and Eric were thrilled when their son, Charlie, was born. They were committed to establishing a family different from the ones in which they had been raised. In Angie's case, that meant providing a sense of cohesiveness and connection that had been lacking in her own family of origin; her mother was an alcoholic and painfully disengaged, leaving Angie and her sisters largely to fend for themselves. Eric's parents were involved, but overly so, controlling Eric's and his sister's activities and as he put it, robbing them of their voice. Both Angie and Eric were determined to give their children the combination of freedom and attention they had missed out on during their own childhoods.

As Charlie grew, Angie and Eric delighted in his big personality. But he had a feisty temperament, making him easily frustrated and difficult to soothe; as a toddler he had full-blown tantrums when he couldn't have his way. Because they wanted to be compassionate and caring, his parents tried to explain to little Charlie why he couldn't have what he wanted, but it only made things worse. And despite being excited about going to "big boy school," he did not do well with the restrictions imposed on him when he started preschool. It was nearly impossible to sit still at story time, and his poor impulse control meant that whenever a child had a toy he wanted, Charlie simply took it — grabbing or shoving as needed.

Soon after he was enrolled, Angie and Eric were called in to speak with the preschool director about an incident in which Charlie had forcefully pushed another child. This meeting turned out to be the first of many related to Charlie's difficulties in managing his behavior. The arrival of a baby sister when he was four only escalated his meltdowns. His parents tried to be understanding, but they were clueless about how to handle their temperamental son — pleading, bargaining, threatening, and mostly caving in to his demands. Charlie ran the household with his tirades, and his parents could hardly remember their peaceful preparenting days. They were embarrassed to be the mother and father of one of "those" kids and on edge each morning about what might happen that day with their mercurial son.

Angie and Eric had believed that their commitment to personal growth would somehow translate into having a sweet and easy time raising kids. After all, weren't children influenced by their surroundings? Surely having a calm, loving home with attentive parents would ensure harmony within the family. But such was not the case. Angie's morning meditations became a thing of the past, and as hard as they tried not to, she and Eric often fell into blaming, saying to each other things like, "If you had only handled the incident with Charlie *this* way instead of *that*, today's crisis could have been avoided."

> *Whether parents identify themselves as traveling a path of personal development, or they simply want to raise happy children without drama or power struggles, they often have a difficult time coming to terms with the realities of raising kids, particularly when their child's needs or temperament prove challenging.*

This couple was like many I have worked with over the past thirty years as a teacher, parent coach, and psychotherapist. Whether parents identify themselves as traveling a path of personal development, or they simply want to raise happy children without drama or power struggles, they often have a difficult time coming to terms with the realities of raising kids, particularly when their child's needs or temperament prove challenging.

Even if we have children who are relatively easy to raise, we still have to adapt to putting another being's wants and needs ahead of our own, day in and day out. From sleepless nights to homework battles, we find ourselves having to develop new qualities as we go, such as tolerance, persistence, and the capacity to read the same picture book over and over...and over again. Those who consider themselves spiritually inclined sometimes confess to being mortified by how *un*spiritual they sometimes feel around their children.

Words they never thought they would utter seem to fly out of their mouths — loudly — words that sound anything *but* enlightened!

But like Angie and Eric, we often discover that the child we have is the one who can teach us the most. And that is what *Parenting with Presence* is all about.

We often discover that the child we have is the one who can teach us the most.

We'll come back to Angie and Eric in a later chapter to discover how their challenges with Charlie paved the way for a much healthier parenting experience and how it provided opportunities for both of them to heal unfinished childhood business. For now, allow me to share a little of my own story.

My Parenting Journey

When I was fifteen years old and living in Kansas, my older brother headed off to college, leaving behind a note recommending that I read a book he'd put in my room called *Autobiography of a Yogi* by Paramahansa Yogananda. It sat on my shelf for two years until the day I found myself diving into it, moved by the tale of an Indian man's journey to know the divine.

This unusual book awakened something in me so profound that upon reading the final page, I pedaled my bike to the Prairie Village shopping center, deposited a handful of coins into the pay phone, dialed the headquarters of Yogananda's California foundation, and said, "I want to know God."

For a year or so I meditated in Yogananda's tradition, based on instructions sent weekly in the mail from the Self-Realization Fellowship. I started doing yoga and explored other types of meditation, eventually settling on one that resonated with me, while weaving in other practices that nourished my heart and soul. I relied so much on the peace I experienced in my daily meditation that if I wasn't able to sit in the morning, I would feel out of sorts all day until I could grab some time to go within.

Eighteen years later, I had a baby. My once regular morning routine fell by the wayside as I struggled to balance inner-focused activities with the pragmatics of family life. Whenever I was rigid about my "spiritually uplifting" pursuits, I ended up feeling

> *I had to figure out how not to tolerate but to savor the moments of ordinary life — changing a diaper, reading a story, or cleaning up after a hurricane of boy-play.*

resentful and uptight. I had to figure out how not to *tolerate* but to *savor* the moments of ordinary life — changing a diaper, reading a story, or cleaning up after a hurricane of boy-play.

One day I was in the kitchen, making my son a grilled-cheese sandwich. As I stood beside the stove waiting for the cheese to melt, I fell into an expanded awareness of what was going on in that moment. There, across the room, was a miracle in the form of someone I loved more than the beating of my heart, and I was getting the chance to express my love in the form of a sandwich. I felt intoxicated with gratitude, realizing that what I was feeling did not have to be an isolated experience; I could live more intimately with this kind of openheartedness as I went about the ordinary activities of my day, if I so chose.

Raising a child turned out to be the greatest transformational experience of my life. I sat for meditation as often as I could — rarely, at first, but more often as my son got older. It is an enormous pleasure to drink from my inner well of stillness and joy, and meditation no doubt influences the "me" that shows up for the world. But I also came to understand that living spiritually means leading the life in front of me as fully present to spirit as possible, regardless of what ritual I might have practiced that morning.

In *Parenting with Presence*, I invite you to embark on your own journey of bringing greater peace, joy, and personal transformation to your day-to-day parenting. You will discover strategies to help you navigate the ups and downs of real-life child rearing with more consciousness, and learn how to subdue the triggers that make you lose (or temporarily misplace!) your equanimity. And you'll be invited to explore ways to bring spirituality into your home — even if you are not religiously inclined or have kids who think anything remotely spiritual is "uncool."

Throughout the book I will share some of the qualities I have come to believe are helpful in transforming a child into an adult who is conscious, confident, and caring. Finally, you will learn practical tools to help you parent *with presence*, responding with flexibility and choice instead of reacting out of frustration, anger, or fear.

When our relationship with our children is permeated with our whole-hearted engagement and presence, they are more inclined to turn to us, rather than to their friends, for guidance and support. In addition, children who feel liked, seen, and cherished — just as they are — are naturally more motivated to do what their parents ask; it is human nature to cooperate with those we feel solidly connected to.

Whether you are an avid spiritual practitioner or you simply want to parent more consciously, raising children with greater presence will open you to more of the love, learning, and joy that the adventure of parenting can bring.

I welcome you on this journey! Let's begin.

NOW IT'S YOUR TURN

For this section and the others like it throughout the book, please visit www.SusanStiffelman.com/PWPextras to hear me guiding you through the exercise.

Whenever I do a coaching session with parents, I begin by asking them to imagine hanging up the phone when we've finished, feeling that our time together was well spent. I invite them to consider what would make that true. "Will you feel better because you now have a plan for dealing with a problem or perhaps because you're clearer about what is fueling a particular issue with your child? Or do you imagine you'll be relieved simply because you're more willing to take baby steps toward shifting things in your family rather than believing you have to change everything at once? Perhaps you're more forgiving of yourself or better able to understand why you get triggered by your kids and what you can do to maintain your cool even when things get difficult."

I find that doing this exercise helps my clients clarify what sort of changes they would like to manifest from our work together.

Allow me to ask you to do something similar. Pause for a moment — perhaps closing your eyes or placing your hand over your heart — and imagine yourself closing this book, feeling happy and excited because you've had a breakthrough. Where are you struggling most as a parent that perhaps will have improved as a result of reading *Parenting with Presence*? What is going well that you want to do more of? What would you like to change?

Become conscious of what you would like your ideal parenting life to look like, picturing a more loving, healthy relationship with your child, as well as with yourself. By setting a clear intention or hoped-for outcome, you may find that you will get more from working with the material in this book, particularly if you're willing to jot down a few notes that you can refer to from time to time.

Please use your journal to reflect on what is working in your parenting life and where you would like to stretch, grow, or transform the relationship you have with your child, your co-parenting partner, and yourself.

CHAPTER 1

You're Living with Your Best Teacher

*Parenting is a mirror in which we get to see
the best of ourselves, and the worst; the richest moments
of living, and the most frightening.*

— MYLA AND JON KABAT-ZINN

In India they're called householder yogis — women and men with an unshakable commitment to their spiritual path who have decided to have a family rather than live in a cave or an ashram. They choose to grow and evolve through their experiences at home and in the workplace, embracing the challenges of everyday life as the means to their transformation.

Many of us subscribe to the belief that spiritual growth happens as a result of daily meditation, mindfulness retreats, and inspiration from wise luminaries. But one of the greatest teachers you could ever hope to learn from is living right under your roof, even if (*especially* if) he or she pushes your buttons or challenges your limitations.

In parenting, things get very real, very fast. Figuring out how to cope when your child spills juice on the new sofa or managing your reactions when your kids tease each other nonstop on the long

> *One of the greatest teachers you could ever hope to learn from is living right under your roof, even if (especially if) he or she pushes your buttons or challenges your limitations.*

9

ride to Grandma's is the equivalent of an advanced course in personal growth. Do you fall apart, or are you able to stay present, deepening your ability to be with "what is," responding rather than reacting?

True spirituality doesn't happen in a cave at the top of a mountain. It's down here, wiping a runny nose, playing yet another round of *Candyland*, or rocking a colicky baby at two in the morning. The Buddha is crying in the next room. How you handle that is as evolved and as spiritual as it gets.

> The Buddha is crying in the next room. How you handle that is as evolved and as spiritual as it gets.

What Is a Teacher?

Many of us are charmed by the image of our sons and daughters as divinely appointed teachers who can help us transform our hearts and souls. But while the idea of seeing our child as one of our teachers has a lyrical, enlightened ring to it, there's a difference between accepting the *idea* of something and embracing the *reality* of it.

Our children may indeed catalyze a love within us that we could not have imagined possible. But they can also elicit powerful elements of our shadow selves, calling forth aspects of our nature, such as impatience and intolerance, that leave us ashamed and overwhelmed.

Maintaining equilibrium is key to living in the moment, but nothing tests our ability to stay centered like parenting. Raising kids can be anything *but* peaceful, with sibling squabbles, homework meltdowns, and arguments over video games all-too-familiar features of the landscape of family life. It's easy for soulful principles to collide with the realities of day-to-day life with children underfoot. Even the most seasoned meditator or yogini may find herself shouting, threatening, bribing, or punishing, despite having set intentions to remain loving and calm no matter what.

There is a saying, *When the student is ready, the teacher appears.* I have long found it to be true that when I am ready to expand my horizons intellectually, psychologically, or spiritually, an opportunity presents itself that seems divinely orchestrated to allow me to stretch, grow, and learn. That said, I don't always *want* to stretch, grow, and learn! Instead, I may feel as if I've been involuntarily enrolled in a class I had no desire to take!

When it comes to parenting, it seems that although we may not have *knowingly* signed up for the "course" our children offer, we nonetheless find ourselves forced ("invited?" "given the opportunity?") to profoundly grow, and grow up. In this respect, I believe our children *can* become our greatest teachers. While we may not deliberately choose to have a baby so that we can heal wounds from our childhood or become a better version of ourselves, in fact, those opportunities — and thousands more — are birthed right along with our children.

We may be confronted with our impatience, taught to slow down as our toddler requires us to stop and smell *every* flower along the sidewalk. Or we may learn fortitude as we survive our child's nightmares, discovering that we actually can be reasonably kind and loving after a series of sleepless nights.

Of equal importance are the ways our children help us work through unfinished business. We may recognize less desirable aspects of ourselves in our child's procrastination around homework, becoming aware — if we're willing — that we are equally guilty of putting off some of our more unpleasant tasks. Or we might feel that we're looking in a mirror when our easily frustrated child launches into meltdowns whenever things don't go his way. There we are in living color, reliving moments from our past (perhaps as recent as this morning!) when we fell apart because we couldn't have our way.

Sometimes the lessons we learn from our children are gentle and sweet; our little ones expand our capacity to give and receive more love and happiness than we ever imagined possible. But often, aspects of our child's temperament challenge us to the core. We may project our own needs onto our children, feeling that we're in battle mode from morning to night when we cannot force them to behave in ways that quell our fear and anxiety. We fall into bed exhausted at the end of each day, dreading the next morning when we have to wake up and do it all over again.

One of the ways I choose to see challenging people as essential to my evolution is to imagine the two of us in a preincarnated state — disembodied souls feeling only pure, limitless love for each other. (This is just an idea; you don't need to believe in reincarnation to benefit from it. Just play along with me for a moment, and see if the image is useful.)

I picture the two of us having a conversation (in whatever way two disembodied beings might converse!) in which we each share what we want to learn in our upcoming life. "I want to learn patience," one of us says. "Well, I would like to deepen my ability to receive love and care," says our soul friend. "How about this? I will come back as your disabled child. I'll learn to accept love more fully, and you will have the chance to learn patience." "It's a deal!" And thus begins what Caroline Myss, lecturer and intuitive, refers to as a *sacred contract*, an agreement we have with the significant people in our lives orchestrating the precise circumstances that will allow us to become more fully who we are meant to be.

> *Each of our children offers us opportunities to confront the dark and dusty corners of our minds and hearts, creating just the right conditions to call forth the kind of learning that can liberate us from old paradigms, allowing us to lead more expansive and fulfilling lives.*

Each of our children offers us opportunities to confront the dark and dusty corners of our minds and hearts, creating just the right conditions to call forth the kind of learning that can liberate us from old paradigms, allowing us to lead more expansive and fulfilling lives. What follows is the story of one such dynamic between a parent and her daughter.

Just Make the Request

Catherine had two daughters, fourteen-year-old Ella and sixteen-year-old Shay. "I get along well with both of my girls — we're very close. But to put it frankly, Shay is a bit of a slob. She drops her towels on the bathroom floor, leaves clothes scattered all over her room, and never washes her dishes without being reminded. This behavior *really* pushes my buttons. We've talked about it, but unless I nag her, she doesn't clean up after herself."

Catherine continued, "Yesterday I asked Shay very nicely if she would tidy up her room before guests came for dinner. She barely looked at me while I was talking and then rolled her eyes and said, 'Mom — they aren't even going to come in my room! Loosen up! You're so uptight when we have people over.' I blew my stack; I do so much for her! Why couldn't she do this one little thing for me?"

I listened for a while and then asked Catherine, "How did your parents respond to you when you expressed a wish or a need? Did they listen and validate your requests, or did they disregard them?"

Immediately, she had an answer. With a hint of sarcasm she replied, "When I had a need? I wasn't *allowed* to have needs. That didn't happen in our family. If I bothered to tell my mother or father that I didn't want to do what they were telling me to do, they pretty much looked at me like I was crazy, telling me how selfish I was. I learned early on to not ask for what I wanted and

have stayed in the passenger seat in all my important relationships, including my marriage."

I told Catherine that I wanted to offer an analogy. "You know
what bumper cars are, the ones at amusement parks, right? Well,
what I've noticed is that some kids get into their little car and
freeze. They've never been behind the wheel of an automobile,
and they don't understand the concept of making it move by stepping on the accelerator, so they just sit in the middle of the track
and get slammed into by all the other wild drivers.

"Then there are the kids at the other extreme. These are the
ones who put the pedal to the floor and never let up. Whichever
direction they turn that steering wheel, they'll be crashing into
something within seconds. In both cases, these young drivers don't
know how to *appropriately* press on the gas. Either they don't move
at all, or they recklessly fling themselves full speed ahead."

I explained that many people struggle to ask for what they
want or need. "Some of us remain passively silent; we don't ask
for anything, feeling unseen, unimportant, and resentful."

"That's me," she offered. "That's the story of my life, from
childhood on through my marriage and divorce. I learned early
on that asking for what I wanted was only going to upset the people around me."

"Other people demand what they want with guns blazing," I
replied. "They overpower those around them, determined to get
their way, regardless of how badly they alienate others.

"So," I said, "would you be willing to look at this situation
with your daughter from a different perspective? Could you see
her as a teacher who is providing you with an excellent assignment? Might you be ready to learn how to ask for what you want
in a way that reflects an understanding that your wishes are as
valid as those of the people around you?"

Catherine was quiet. All traces of sarcasm were gone as she

softly said, "Wow. Yes. It's time for me to learn to ask for what I need."

I replied, "By looking at why your child's behavior triggers you so deeply, you have an opportunity to heal something from long ago and grow into a more healthy and whole version of yourself."

Catherine was on board. Our work together shifted from "fixing" her daughter's messiness to healing the sadness she felt as a little girl who had concluded that her desires and needs were not important — feelings she had buried long ago. I helped her understand that the intensity with which she had been coming at Shay to get her to cooperate was a result of projecting onto her daughter an unresolved longing to know that her own wishes and wants mattered.

I explained that it isn't our children's job to fix us. In fact, they often dig in their heels when we come at them with our neediness and desperation. Intuitively, they understand that it isn't their responsibility to behave in ways that heal whatever wounds we bring from earlier relationships. So it can happen that our children's misbehavior truly *does* become a gift, because if we are willing to look within instead of projecting our hurts onto them, we can work through unfinished emotional business.

> *Intuitively, our children understand that it isn't their responsibility to behave in ways that heal whatever wounds we bring from earlier relationships. So it can happen that our children's misbehavior truly does become a gift, because if we are willing to look within instead of projecting our hurts onto them, we can work through unfinished emotional business.*

I encouraged Catherine to simply be present with whatever feelings came up for her when she was met with her daughter's resistance. "Practice nonjudgmental awareness, allowing room for whatever emotions have gotten stirred up so they can have their say. Be sad or angry. Be confused or worried. And then, perhaps, be sad again. Let feelings move through you without censoring or controlling them.

"Locate where in your body you are experiencing what you're feeling. Is the sensation heavy? Sharp? Fluttery? Simply allow whatever you are experiencing to *be*, without making the emotions bigger or smaller. Name the feelings with loving-kindness. 'There's sadness in my chest. It's heavy and flat and dark. And now there's anger. So sharp and hard. All through my body!'

"Avoid your left, rational brain's attempts to explain away your discomfort. Resist the urge to make it about your daughter or the specific situation. Simply notice what you're experiencing. Be patient. The emotions will pass through. You *will* feel better. The only way out is through. It is a process of grieving for the voice you didn't have, the empathy you didn't receive, and the hurt of having felt invisible."

This was — and is — a very deep process. It isn't easy or quick. Old wounds need breathing room to heal. As you move through this process, I encourage you to be kind and patient with yourself, even as you begin trying new ways of dealing with your child when she activates an old hurt. With care, you can start to heal the dynamic, and yourself.

Once Catherine allowed herself to grieve for the parts of her that had been afraid to express her wishes, she was ready to try new ways of asking things of her girls. I shared with her something I once heard Diane Sawyer say when she was asked about the success of her long marriage. She replied, "I learned early on that a criticism is just a really lousy way of making a request. So... just make the request!"

The Four Modalities of Interaction

In our interactions with others, we generally fall into one of four categories. We are either passive, aggressive, passive-aggressive, or assertive.

We are in *passive* mode when we suppress what we truly feel, pretending that everything is okay. When we are passive, we say yes when we mean no, put others' needs ahead of our own, and are terrified of ruffling anyone's feathers. Passive parents are afraid of their children's upset and desperately want to be liked by them, so they give in to their demands.

When we are *aggressive*, we come *at* our children using threats and intimidation to bend them to our will. It may look effective on the outside — the misbehavior stops — but this approach comes at a high price. Our children cannot feel close to us because we are not emotionally safe.

Passive-aggressive parents control their children through shame and guilt. They may not be overtly aggressive, but their subtle guilt trips and manipulations are extremely harmful to their children's developing sense of self. These kids feel inappropriately responsible for their parents' needs and happiness rather than in tune with their own. If you say, "You're the only child in this family who can't seem to figure out how to set the table right," you have just shamed your child. Telling her, "I didn't sleep a wink last night, worrying about how I'm going to pay for that class trip you insist you have to go on," she can't help but feel guilty. These are very unhealthy ways of interacting with children.

We are *assertive* when we are being what I call the Captain of the ship in our children's lives. (More on this in chapter 2.) In this mode, we maintain healthy boundaries with our children, allowing them to have their needs, wants, feelings, and preferences without making them wrong when they don't nicely overlap with our own. We don't *need* our children to like us, and we are not afraid of their unhappiness, recognizing that if we fix all their problems we are impairing their ability to develop true resilience. Our children know that they are loved for who they are, not for what they can do for us or how their achievements make us look to others.

And when we are assertive, we can acknowledge that our children may not want to do what we ask, without taking their complaints personally or escalating the disagreement into a power struggle. We empathize with their position, allowing them to feel what they feel, but we are not reluctant to set limits that might disappoint them.

> *When we are assertive, we can acknowledge that our children may not want to do what we ask, without taking their complaints personally or escalating the disagreement into a power struggle.*

My work with Catherine first focused on helping her grieve for the sweet and loving childhood she never had. It was vulnerable work, but she was committed and moved through her old feelings bravely.

Then we started practicing assertiveness. Since she had almost no experience with assertive behavior in either her childhood or her marriage, this was uncharted territory for her. But we had a lot of fun; we role-played scenarios in which she was able to practice expressing her wishes in a way that wasn't aggressive (pressing the accelerator to the floor), passive (staying frozen and still), or passive-aggressive (using shame or put-downs). Catherine loved how she felt when she assertively voiced her needs.

As a result of working through this emotional baggage, Catherine's requests lost their edginess and desperation, making it easier for Shay to agree to what her mother was asking of her. Catherine practiced coming *alongside* her daughter (what I call Act 1 Parenting) by letting Shay know that she understood that she might not think it was a big deal if she left her clothes strewn around her room. "You might even think that since it's *your* room, you should have the right to things the way you want them." Because Shay felt understood and validated by her mom, she was less defensive and more receptive.

"Unfortunately, sweetheart," her assertive mom went on,

"since it does bother *me* to come into your room and see clothes everywhere, and I'm the one paying the rent, I'd like you to make more of an effort to keep it clean. I want you to spend five or ten minutes putting things away each night before you climb into bed. And it will be great if you would make sure that you leave the bathroom the way you found it — which means that your towels find their way into the hamper!"

Before Catherine discovered what lay buried beneath her heightened sensitivity to this issue with her daughter, either she kept her foot off the gas (passively saying nothing but teeming with repressed anger and resentment), or she slammed on the accelerator (aggressively coming at her daughter with criticism and anger).

By choosing to see her daughter as a wonderful teacher who was providing her with an assignment to reclaim her voice and to respectfully ask for what she needed, Catherine began to feel even closer to Shay. And the house was tidier, too!

NOW IT'S YOUR TURN

In your journal, write your child's name. Below it, note a quality in your child that is particularly difficult for you to deal with — a characteristic or behavior that pushes your buttons and causes you to react intensely, meaning you get extremely upset when others might just feel mildly annoyed. Avoid censoring yourself; be truthful.

Here are some examples: *impatient, messy, bossy, self-centered, highly sensitive, inflexible, overly cautious, rude, negative, superficial, aggressive, shy, immature. Sneaky, picky, provocative, easily frustrated, sassy, scattered, judgmental, unaffectionate, stubborn, controlling, unappreciative, overly rational, hypochondriacal, argumentative, unmotivated, weak, timid, persistent, complaining, gives up easily, whiny, hyper, restless, won't accept no for an answer, procrastinator, doesn't follow through.*

Now answer these questions, focusing on the ones that apply to you. Take your time; sometimes it takes a little while to locate the truth beneath our knee-jerk interpretation of what's going on.

- Who in your past does your child remind you of when she exhibits this behavior? A parent or teacher? Big brother or little sister? Former spouse?
- How did you cope when this person manifested this behavior or trait? Did you withdraw? Did you become aggressive? Did you argue? Throw a tantrum? Hide? Cry? Were you passive? Aggressive? Passive-aggressive?
- How did this person respond to your problems or complaints? Did he blame you for your challenges? Did he dismiss or trivialize your concerns? Tell you that you were overreacting? Did he punish you for tattling? Tell you to work out your problems on your own? Make you feel guilty for speaking up? Tell you how much harder *his*

life was than yours? Ridicule you for being too sensitive?

- Is your child expressing an undesirable trait that reminds you of something *in yourself* you find hard to face? Do you do the very thing that you find unacceptable in your child? What feelings come up for you as you explore the ways you and your child share a tendency to express this quality?

- How did your early caregivers interact with you when you manifested this unpleasant trait or behavior? Were they critical or shaming? Did they compare you to a more agreeable sibling? Were you isolated or sent to your room to "think about how you have been bad?" Did a parent withhold his or her love? Shout and threaten? Physically hurt you?

- What are you grieving as a result of your child having this particular characteristic? What quality is being called forth from you to meet your child exactly as she is? What are you being invited to learn? Is your child gifting you with the chance to learn more patience? Self-acceptance? Assertiveness? Flexibility?

Peering beneath the surface of behaviors in our child that trigger unresolved feelings within our hearts and minds is deep work and not to be taken lightly. If emotions bubble to the surface that are difficult to process on your own, please seek the support of a trusted friend or a trained therapist.

If, like Catherine, you choose to see your child as your teacher and to embrace the healing and transformation that is being offered, the rewards can be limitless.

MAKING IT PRACTICAL
Parenting with Presence in Real Life

How can I keep from being bugged by my child's whining?

QUESTION: My four-year-old's whining drives me crazy. I know she's little and can't always put her wishes into words, but for some reason her whiny voice sends me through the roof!

SUGGESTION: You are not alone. There is something about a child's high-pitched wail that can set a parent's teeth on edge. But becoming reactive only makes the problem worse.

Try viewing your daughter's whining as a completely neutral event. Just as with a child who persistently taps his pencil or kicks his foot, these behaviors aren't inherently good or bad. What makes them annoying is that we *decide* that they are, which sets us up for a power struggle. If you need your child to stop doing something because you decide it's irritating, then unless your connection is very strong, you are likely to provoke her into persisting.

It may sound very Zen-like, but if you can move into a place of *noticing* rather than labeling or *judging* her whiny voice, you will be able to say, "Sweetheart, I want to hear what you need, and I'm happy to wait until you can use your regular voice." When you are less reactive, your daughter should be able to figure out how to appropriately ask for what she wants.

What is my sassy tween teaching me?

QUESTION: My eleven-year-old rolls her eyes or mimics me when I ask her to do something. I find this behavior very disrespectful. What could I be learning from having to deal with a sassy tween?

SUGGESTION: How much time do you have? The things we can learn from our sassy tweens could fill volumes! Let's start with *not taking things personally.*

There is a notable lack of positive role models for youngsters your daughter's age, who are desperately trying to figure out how to step into adolescence and start individuating from their parents. Unfortunately, many take on the snarky behavior of kids on popular TV shows, where eye rolling and talking back is rewarded with an enthusiastic laugh track.

Refuse to make your daughter's eye rolling mean more than what it is — an awkward and (hopefully) ineffective way of announcing that she doesn't feel like doing what you've asked or that she is testing your limits. If you can refrain from taking it personally, you'll be able to simply say, "Why don't you take a do-over on that one, honey" — hopefully, without a sassy tone in *your* voice!

What am I learning from being ignored?

QUESTION: I have a fifteen-year-old son who treats me as if I don't exist. He walks in the door and heads straight to his room without even saying hello. What could he possibly be teaching me?

SUGGESTION: Alas, child rearing can be brutal, especially for those who have unfinished business around having felt invisible, unimportant, or unpopular. The good news is that by approaching these experiences consciously, we are able not only to parent more effectively but also to heal some of our own childhood wounds.

Be *present* with what you're experiencing instead of focusing on how to change your son. If you have a physical reaction — tension, anger — be friendly toward the sensations without making them bigger or smaller. Name them — *there's clenching...in my belly...like a knot that's getting tighter.*

If your reaction is more emotional, stay present with what your feelings bring up. *There's sadness...reminds me of feeling invisible in middle school...I hated how kids ignored me at lunch...*

While each person will have a unique set of feelings that come up when they start being more present with what gets triggered by their kids, my recommendation is the same. Start with what's going on *within you* before taking on the issue with your child. Only then will you be able to address the problem as the Captain of the ship, without infusing it with neediness.

CHAPTER 2

Growing Up
While Raising Kids

*It is easier to build strong children
than to repair broken men.*

— FREDERICK DOUGLASS

Years ago I was driving my son to school when another parent, headed for the same destination, had a diabetic seizure. Realizing that his unconscious mother would not be able to prevent the car from careening out of control, her eleven-year-old son unhooked his seat belt and attempted to steer the car to safety. When he realized that he couldn't figure out what to do, he frantically belted himself back in just seconds before their Suburban hit four cars — including ours. His mother woke up when she crashed into a guardrail. Thankfully, none of the eleven people involved in the accident was badly hurt.

> *Children don't want to be in charge; it's just that they know somebody has to be, because they understand that life is not safe unless someone competent is behind the wheel.*

Children are meant to be passengers. They aren't equipped to drive a car or sail a ship through storms — and they know it. But when no one is in the driver's seat, they instinctively try to take over. They don't *want* to be in charge; it's just that they know somebody has to be, because they understand that life is not safe unless someone competent is behind the wheel.

25

Captain, Lawyer, Dictator

In my book *Parenting Without Power Struggles,* I described three ways that parents can engage with their children: being confidently and calmly in charge, negotiating for power, or fighting their child for control.

CAPTAIN —	**TWO LAWYERS —**	**DICTATOR —**
PARENT IN CHARGE	**NO ONE IN CHARGE**	**CHILD IN CHARGE**

Parents who are calmly and confidently in charge as the Captain of the ship come across as clear, loving, and capable of making good decisions on behalf of their children — even if those decisions upset their kids because they can't have what they want. When we are captaining the ship, we are responsively flexible, *choosing* how we engage with our child during one of his storms rather than reflexively *reacting* based on triggered behaviors we inherited from our own upbringing.

> *Parents who are calmly and confidently in charge, being Captain of the ship, come across as clear, loving, and capable of making good decisions on behalf of their children, even if those decisions upset their kids because they can't do or have what they want.*

Here is a brief example. Your thirteen-year-old asks if she can go to a party where the only supervision will be an older sister who is not known for her good judgment.

MOM: "Honey, I know you want to go, but unfortunately, I don't feel it's a good idea."

DAUGHTER: "Please, Mom? I promise nothing bad will happen."

MOM: "Oh, sweetheart. I know it doesn't seem fair, and I know how much you want to go, but I'm afraid not."

Mom is being the *Captain*, demonstrating empathy and kindness while remaining decisive and clear. Depending on how accustomed your child is to you changing your mind or waffling, she may attempt to draw you into the next way of interacting.

When parents engage in quarrels, power struggles, and negotiations with their kids, no one is in charge. I call this mode the Two Lawyers. Kids push against their parents, parents push against their kids, and the relationship is fraught with tension and resentment. Here's an example:

> *When parents engage in quarrels, power struggles, and negotiations with their kids, no one is in charge.*

DAUGHTER: "Mom, you treat me like I'm a two-year-old. You never trust me!"

MOM: "You're never happy unless you get what you want! Carey's sister is immature, and I don't trust her to keep an eye on you guys. She'll probably just have a party of her own! In fact, last year I heard that she..." Mom argues for her position, and her child argues right back.

DAUGHTER: "That's *so* not true! She was blamed for smoking pot in the school bathroom, but she wasn't even smoking! She just happened to be there when those *other* girls were doing it!"

These kind of parent-child interactions are characterized by fighting, arguing, and bargaining.

Finally, when the child is the one calling the shots, the parents feel out of control and even panicked, especially if they imagine that others are judging them for not managing their kids well. They try to restore order and control by overpowering their children with threats, bribes, or ultimatums, similar to how a tyrant or despot — having no authentic authority — asserts control through fear and intimidation. I call this mode the *Dictator*. Here's an example:

DAUGHTER: "You just can't accept that I'm not your little baby anymore. Why don't you get a life, so you can stop trying to control mine?"

MOM: "That's it, young lady. You never appreciate all the things we do for you. I work hard just to put food on the table, and you never even say thank you. You're grounded!"

As you can see, this situation rapidly deteriorates, with mom quickly losing her footing and shifting from Captain to Lawyer and, finally, entering Dictator mode.

Staying in Captain mode requires that we become comfortable setting limits so that we can parent with kindness, clarity, and confidence.

> *Staying in Captain mode requires that we become comfortable setting limits so that we can parent with kindness, clarity, and confidence.*

Setting Limits

In my counseling practice, I often see well-meaning couples who are committed to avoiding the mistakes their own parents made, yet who confess to having a tremendous lack of confidence when it comes to handling challenging situations. "Is it okay if I let my fourteen-year-old experiment with smoking pot? His friends are all trying it." "I tried to cancel my son's *World of Warcraft* subscription, but he got so furious he punched a hole in the wall!" "My kids become little terrors when we go out to eat unless I turn my cell phone over to them. Should I give in to keep the peace?" Unsure of themselves and afraid to set limits, they convey to their children that they don't know where they stand, or perhaps more accurately, that they are simply afraid to *take* a stand, lest they upset their children.

What I find interesting is that the very kids who have outbursts when they don't get their way almost always long for their parents to create some real connection and structure. Sometimes, when I meet privately with youngsters like these, they tell me that they wish their parents weren't so wishy-washy. And other times, they make this known simply by responding positively when someone combines limit setting with deep and secure attachment. Henry was one such child.

> *The very kids who have outbursts when they don't get their way almost always long for their parents to create some real connection and structure.*

Forging a Real Connection

Henry was eleven when Bradley and Melissa brought him to see me. He sauntered into my office playing his portable game player (this was a few years ago) and dripping with attitude. When his parents meekly suggested that he put the device down and greet me, he glared at them and continued to play. When I met with them alone, they admitted to being clueless about how to handle their son's severe meltdowns. Raised by an older father who believed boys should be tough, Henry had learned to stifle his more tender feelings from a young age and had lost his ability to feel emotions such as fear, sadness, and hurt; his repertoire was limited to frustration and anger. Henry was a big child and could turn violent when provoked. His parents were terrified of him.

When I met alone with Henry, however, I found him to be a gentle but very ungrounded child. He seemed to be floating above himself, unaccustomed to full contact with a caring grown-up who didn't want anything from him. The majority of his adult interactions consisted of people trying to coerce him to do things he didn't want to do.

I began by showing an interest in discovering who Henry

was. As we talked, he tentatively opened up, telling me how much he loved drawing and about his dream of designing video games. When I noticed that he kept splitting his attention between our conversation and his gaming device, I asked him — in a friendly way — to hand it to me, explaining that it seemed as though it had a particularly strong hold on him. I put the device on a shelf in my office, where it remained for many months, with a surprising degree of acceptance.

Henry and I began to forge a real connection. I was steady in my kindness and interest, and he slowly began to trust that I was his ally. I found the coaching sessions with his parents more challenging. Melissa and Bradley were resistant to doing the work of applying what we spoke about in our sessions — coming *alongside* rather than *at* Henry. Again and again they used logic, bribes, or threats to compel him to do what they wanted. It seemed as if they were more invested in having me change their son so he would just do what they asked rather than in improving the quality of their relationship with him.

Early one evening, my phone rang. It was Bradley, calling me from the parking lot of a restaurant, distraught. Apparently, Henry had had a major tantrum in the restaurant and had fled to the parking lot, where he was dodging his parents. Bradley and Melissa were desperately trying to corral their son into the car so they could head home. "Will you talk to Henry? Will you convince him to get into the car?" Bradley pleaded.

It was an unusual request, but I agreed, not knowing quite what I was going to be up against. But this is how it went down: Bradley got close enough to Henry to tell him that Susan was on the phone and that she wanted to talk to him. Henry took the phone right away. I simply said, "Sweetheart, it's time to get into the car."

"Okay."

That was it. He handed the phone back to his father and got in the car.

What did I do that his parents couldn't have done? What power did I have over Henry that made him say yes? None. But I did have two things: an authentic connection with him — he knew that I liked, enjoyed, and respected him — and legitimate standing as the Captain of the ship in our relationship. I wasn't afraid of him, I didn't need him to bolster my sense of self-worth, and I had proved that I genuinely cared about him. He knew that I was on his side.

How had I accomplished this? By listening to Henry with full presence, accepting him as he was. He knew that I found him funny and interesting. He knew that I had no ulterior motive; I didn't *need* anything from him. So he responded positively to my request, as we are inclined to do when a person we like asks something of us.

Sadly, the only time Henry was given his parent's complete attention was either when they were trying to convince him to do something he did not want to do — finishing homework, taking a shower, coming to dinner — or when they wanted him to stop doing something that he *did* want to do, such as playing video games or enjoying the coziness of his warm bed in the morning. Rarely did they invest time in getting to know their son as a person — not because they were lacking in love, but because like many parents, they were driven and distracted by the demands and stressors of their busy lives. As a result, Henry felt no allegiance to his parents, making him minimally invested in pleasing them. In the absence of any reservoir of goodwill with Henry, they felt forced to bribe or threaten him to elicit his cooperation.

Healing Your Unfinished Business

You may recall Angie and Eric from the introduction, where I described how the realities of raising their temperamental child had collided with the blissful picture they had envisioned of their conscious parenting lives. My work with them began when their son, Charlie, was four and a half. They came to see me because Charlie had been threatened with suspension from preschool for his aggressive behavior. They had also reached their limit at home, where their son's outbursts had established a climate of constant chaos and tension.

I began by exploring Angie and Eric's internal conflicts around setting limits. Both parents were uncertain about how, when, or where they should draw the line with little Charlie. In Eric's case, his lack of clarity was a result of having been raised by overly restrictive parents who controlled his every move. He was determined to provide his children with the freedom to make their own choices. As a result, he admitted to often erring on the side of setting unclear guidelines for his son.

We spoke about the idea of dampening a child's spirit. "Eric, it sounds as though you are passionate about wanting your children to have their voice and to be free to express their wishes." He nodded, affirming that this was something he felt strongly about. I asked him to talk about what it had been like for him growing up, and he spoke about how overpowered he felt by his parents, who dictated his every move. "If they wanted me to take piano lessons, I had to take them — and practice every day. I didn't *like* the piano, but that didn't matter. It was their way or the highway. Same with what clothes I wore, what TV shows I watched, which sports activities I took part in — I had no way of asserting my will in my family. I felt weak and powerless, and I'm determined not to raise my kids that way." Wisely, Eric understood that his children were separate and unique individuals, not meant to be the agents of his own unfulfilled dreams.

But Eric's unfinished business was having a negative impact on how he was raising his son. "Unfortunately, because this was such a significant hurt for you growing up, you run the risk of overcompensating for the strictness of your parents by being so unstructured with Charlie that it is actually hurting him."

I told them that I encounter this predicament a lot, particularly with parents who take their personal growth or spiritual practices very seriously. I have great admiration for those who are committed to conscious parenting — empowering their children to speak their minds and hearts and to trust their feelings and intuitions. But we have to provide them with structure and not be afraid of establishing limits. Given how badly things had deteriorated with Charlie, Eric was open to considering that there might be a way to be more assertive with Charlie *without* crushing his spirit.

> *I have great admiration for those who are committed to conscious parenting — empowering their children to speak their minds and hearts and to trust their feelings and intuitions. But we have to provide them with structure and not be afraid of establishing limits.*

Angie, triggered when her son's tantrums reminded her of her mother's unpredictable and explosive rages, found it easier to cave in to Charlie's demands than to set boundaries. And the constant tension he created meant that she found herself less eager to spend time with him, plopping him down in front of an iPad or TV screen, where he wouldn't make any trouble. But little Charlie pushed for contact with his mother, even if it required misbehaving. He had discovered that acting out was a way to ensure receiving 100 percent of her attention. In some respects, he was a little Henry in the making.

Essentially, Charlie needed to find out if his parents were capable of creating a container within which he could safely explore the world. His behavior was in effect an announcement that he didn't feel safe sailing the seas of his life in the absence of a competent Captain. As a result, whenever Charlie experienced frustration, he felt the need to fling himself on the floor, throw things, or kick and hit his parents.

I explained the three modes of parenting and the importance of stepping into the role of Captain of the ship. They both agreed that they mostly lived in Dictator mode — letting Charlie call the shots and have his way until things got so awful that they would threaten severe punishment to snap him back to his senses.

But resorting to anger was unaligned with their more spiritual values, leaving them feeling guilty and remorseful. And thus the cycle was perpetuated — enduring their son's tirades until they reached their tipping point, exploding at him, then feeling shame about their inability to stay calm and centered.

I shared with Angie and Eric what Eckhart Tolle refers to as the "pain-body" — residual emotional pain that feeds off negativity. He writes, "While the child is having a pain-body attack, there isn't much you can do except to stay present so that you are not drawn into an emotional reaction. The child's pain-body would only feed on it. Pain-bodies can be extremely dramatic. Don't buy into the drama. Don't take it too seriously. If the pain-body was triggered by thwarted wanting, don't give in now to its demands. Otherwise, the child will learn: 'The more unhappy I become, the more likely I am to get what I want.' " Tolle suggests that when a child is having a meltdown, it is an unconscious attempt on the part of their pain-body to strengthen itself by pulling others into drama and misery.

Whether or not this language is familiar to you, the idea

> "While the child is having a pain-body attack, there isn't much you can do except to stay present so that you are not drawn into an emotional reaction.... Don't take it too seriously. If the pain-body was triggered by thwarted wanting, don't give in now to its demands. Otherwise, the child will learn: 'The more unhappy I become, the more likely I am to get what I want.' "

probably make sense. When we take our child's misbehavior personally, our ego gets involved, generating desperation or a need for control, pulling out all the stops to assert itself. Once this dynamic is in play, we are inevitably going to move into Lawyer or Dictator mode because, in a sense, the ego has committed mutiny, hijacking the Captain and the calm leadership that would otherwise ensure smooth sailing through a child's storm.

Being Clear, Connected, and Present

The one person Charlie seemed to behave well with was his babysitter. Alison was in her midtwenties and had no children but had been raised in a large, close-knit family. She exuded a kind of no-nonsense attitude that made it clear that she was comfortable being in charge. She and Charlie had a very playful and loving relationship, but when she told him to brush his teeth or stop teasing his sister, he almost always cooperated. I suspected that there were a number of reasons Charlie was able to manage his behavior with Alison. First, she didn't take his behavior personally; she was not invested in his being a "good boy" the way Angie and Eric were and was therefore less desperate or needy when she interacted with him. In other words, Charlie was not the means by which she proved that she was a good or competent person.

But there was more to it than that. As Angie talked about Alison's relationship with her son, it was obvious that Alison *enjoyed* Charlie. They laughed a lot when they were together, and Alison invested plenty of time meeting him exactly where he was — playing with robots, building forts, or just chasing each other around the yard. Whereas most of Angie's interactions with her son were focused on getting things checked off a list — breakfast, dressing for school, taking a bath — Alison slowed down and was genuinely *present* with Charlie. She listened attentively when he made up a story about his dinosaurs, asking questions and taking obvious pleasure in his vivid imagination. She kept her cell phone muted when they were having special playtime so Charlie didn't feel he was constantly competing with outside people intruding on their time, as he did with his parents. Alison had fun with Charlie at least a little bit each day, making it clear that she liked him, an essential ingredient in catalyzing a child's willingness to cooperate.

Alison was consistently making deposits in her emotional bank account with Charlie, giving him heartfelt doses of pure presence, focus, and attention. Every friendly interaction was like depositing a coin in the "account" of their relationship, making it easy for her to make what might feel to Charlie like "withdrawals" when she wanted him to comply with a request. Charlie was more inclined to cooperate with Alison, not because he was afraid of being punished by her but because he wanted to please her, knowing she genuinely cared for him.

> *It felt good for Charlie to be cooperative with Alison, not because he was afraid of being punished by her but because he wanted to please her.*

As Angie and Eric described Alison's communication style, it also became clear that when she made requests of Charlie, she meant business, and he knew it. While he sensed his parent's lack of decisiveness when they told him it was time to come to dinner or put on his shoes, he perceived Alison's delivery as clear, loving, and firm, prompting consent. Her requests didn't end with "...okay?" Rather, she announced what had to be done as the Captain of the ship, remaining compassionate when he voiced his reluctance but unwavering in her clarity.

Angie and Eric admitted to feeling a little jealous of Alison's ability to expect and receive cooperative behavior from Charlie. They tried mimicking her words, but Charlie still resisted. I explained that it wasn't Alison's words that were convincing

Charlie to behave well. When children feel a connection with the person making a request, their instinct to cooperate is awakened, naturally inclining them to comply. Charlie knew that his babysitter enjoyed him, making him *want* to behave well when he was with her.

> *When children feel a connection with the person making a request, their instinct to cooperate is awakened, naturally inclining them to comply.*

Letting Your Child Feel Sad

There was another element I wanted to explore in my work with Angie and Eric: I needed to know how they felt about allowing their son to be sad or disappointed, something I always look at when a child is chronically angry or aggressive. I often observe parents having great difficulty tolerating their child's unhappiness. In fact, there is a quote, "A mother/father is only as happy as their saddest child." While this is a sweet sentiment, it highlights one of the greatest challenges we face: recognizing that our children are separate people on their own life's journey.

I remember a conversation I had with Sally, one of my closest friends, when I realized that my marriage was not likely to survive. I was heartbroken that I couldn't protect my son from what was coming. How could I, a therapist who had seen so many children struggle through their parents' divorces, put my son through that? I said to Sally, "Ari isn't supposed to go through this — the coming apart of his family in this way. He's not supposed to have to deal with this." I will never forget her response. She looked me in the eye and said, "How do *you* know what he's supposed to go through?"

I got it. I understood that although wild horses couldn't stop me from doing my best to provide my son with a good life, he was indeed going to have experiences — difficult ones — that I could not prevent, no matter how hard I tried. The best I could do at those times was to stay lovingly present to him as he traveled through pain and disappointment. Now that he is twenty-four, I can see the ways that he was strengthened and made more compassionate by working through the losses I wanted to protect him from.

This is not to say that I would suggest putting kids through hardships to build character; nothing could be further from the truth. But when we cannot shield our children from painful experiences, the next best thing is to be fully present to them, helping them through the process by letting them feel their sadness and disappointment.

> *When we cannot shield our children from painful experiences, the next best thing is to be fully present to them, helping them through the process by letting them feel their sadness and disappointment.*

There is a poignant scene in the show *Parenthood* that illustrates this beautifully. Max, the fifteen-year-old son of Christina and Adam, struggles to fit in at his high school because his Asperger's has made him an outcast. Blessedly, he has discovered that he has a great talent for taking photographs, resulting in his being assigned the job as yearbook photographer. Unfortunately, he starts snapping pictures of a girl as she is sobbing while surrounded by friends. The girls tell Max to go away, but he insensitively insists that he's supposed to take B-roll shots for the yearbook, and he carries on. Max's parents are called to school for a meeting at which they are informed that Max cannot continue to take yearbook photos; the teacher has reassigned him to layout. They beg the teacher and principal to reconsider, pulling out all the stops in an effort to ensure that their son will have this one satisfying school experience, but the girl's complaints make it impossible for Max to continue.

Christina bears the burden of informing Max that he has lost his position as yearbook photographer. She walks into his room, sits down, and with great anguish, tells her son that he has been moved from photography to layout. "What? I don't want to do layout! I want to be the photographer! I'm the best one for the job!" Christina says, "I know, Max, but the teacher has decided and won't change his mind." Max is furious. None of this makes sense to him; in his mind, he did nothing wrong, and logically, should be taking photos for the yearbook. He says, "What are you going to do about it?" With an aching heart, Christina looks at her son and says simply, "I'm just going to sit here with you and be sad."

I was enormously touched by this scene. Because Christina had moved through her grief around being unable to prevent her son from losing something that mattered so much to him, she was able to be with him as he dealt with letting go of something he wanted so badly. She didn't explain, justify, or even attempt to make him feel better. Instead, she was simply present with him, trusting that the waves of his disappointment would wash over him and then recede and that he would find his way through loss to acceptance.

Helping Children Move through Loss

I knew that because Eric and Angie wanted Charlie to be happy, they routinely gave in to his demands or tried to talk him out of his upset. Not surprisingly, they confessed that their son seldom cried. This little boy would pop with rage if he didn't get his way, but his anger rarely moved on to actual sadness or tears. I asked Angie and Eric to consider what it would be like to not fix Charlie's problems when he was frustrated, instead helping him feel his unhappiness. Imagining this caused them both to feel unsettled. "If I love my son," asked Eric, "how can I not want to make him happy?"

I asked them what they ultimately wanted for Charlie as he headed into adulthood — what skills and resources they hoped he would have internalized that would let them know he was likely to have a good life. "We want him to know how to get along with people and to have a positive attitude that helps him attract good things. And we want him to be able to handle the tough times as well."

I explained that for children to develop the internal resources to accept life on its terms, they must be allowed to move through the stages of *denial, anger,* and *bargaining* when they can't have what they want so that they can then move through their *disappointment* to *acceptance* — an idea I borrowed from Elisabeth Kübler-Ross's work with the dying and that I explain more fully in *Parenting Without Power Struggles.* The acronym for these stages is DABDA.

Angie and Eric's desire to insulate their son from the full weight of his disappointments was keeping Charlie in what I refer to as the DAB — the first three stages of grieving: denial, anger, and bargaining. Because they usually caved in when Charlie's frustration began to escalate, he started out in a state of denial when he asked for something. Understandably, he didn't believe that no really meant no, based on past experiences, so he stayed in denial, unable to accept that *this* time his parents were not going to give in to his demands.

Pushing back at Charlie with matching fury kept him in the stage of anger. Parent and child lobbed reactive, hurtful missiles back and forth at each other, with ever-increasing rage on both sides. When his parents engaged in heated debates about *why* Charlie couldn't have what he wanted, they were fueling the bargaining stage, in effect encouraging their son to argue for whatever he was demanding.

Stepping into the Captain role with Charlie meant they

would need to be anchored firmly enough within themselves to endure his sorrow or disappointment (Kübler-Ross calls this stage "depression"). This was an essential step toward helping Charlie reduce the reservoir of frustration that so easily exploded whenever he encountered something he couldn't change or control. Unless a child can feel sad when he cannot have what he wants, he will never make it to the stage of acceptance.

"What message does Charlie get about your belief in his capacity to handle disappointment when you jump through hoops to prevent him from feeling sad?" I asked. Thinking about it this way made an impact. They began to see that when they fixed Charlie's problems or tried to explain away his upsets, they were in effect telling him they didn't have faith that he had the internal resources to deal with life when it didn't go his way — not a good message to communicate to a child if you're hoping he will become a resilient adult.

Still, Angie was afraid to stand firm with Charlie. Just thinking about it made her tremble inside. "I hate to admit it, but I'm a pushover. I can't imagine standing up to Charlie when he starts heading into one of his tirades. It's like trying to stay upright in the middle of a hurricane!"

I asked her to stand in front of me and picture herself with Charlie when he started revving up to have a meltdown. "Tune in to what is going on in your body." She closed her eyes, got quiet, and then described herself as feeling very young and very shaky. "I feel like a little girl — not strong enough to cope. I want to crawl under a rock and hide." She acknowledged that these were familiar feelings, reminiscent of all the times when

> *They began to see that when they fixed Charlie's problems or tried to explain away his upsets, they were in effect telling him they didn't have faith that he had the internal resources to deal with life when it didn't go his way — not a good message to communicate to a child if you're hoping he will become a resilient adult.*

she had felt too weak to deal with her mother's intensity and chaos. While she was in this state, I told her that I was going to push gently against her. When I did, she instantly lost her balance, catching herself just before she toppled over.

"Now I want you to imagine a steel cable running from the top of your head, down through your body, into the soles of your feet, continuing straight down into the center of the earth. Picture that steel cable as rigid and unwavering. Nothing can make it move or sway. Feel your strength; feel yourself as sturdy as an ancient redwood tree whose roots go deeply down into the ground." As she imagined this, I pushed exactly as hard as I had before. This time, instead of easily losing her balance, she was immovable.

"How did that feel, Angie?"

"It felt great! I felt my strength; I felt solid and steady. Powerful, without having to force myself to resist or be strong. I felt like a grown-up!"

I invited both Angie and Eric to try this exercise a few times, imagining themselves in Charlie's presence when he started skidding into one of his storms, while picturing the steel cable giving them a strong backbone. "Remember, you do him no favors when you modify things to his liking. If you want your son to grow into an adult who can handle things when they don't go his way, you will have to help him develop that muscle of resilience now by staying present with him as he experiences the full weight of his disappointments.

"Go ahead and feel your heavy-heartedness as you accept that you cannot shield Charlie from every frustration or loss, and then picture yourself standing steady, with that cable anchoring you to the earth. Inhabit a gentle but unyielding strength as you acknowledge your son's feelings with love, but allow him to move through his denial, anger, and bargaining so that he simply feels sad."

I worked with this family for about three months. We focused on reducing their discomfort with Charlie's frustrations without feeling the constant need to manipulate things to his liking. We explored their fears about dampening his spirit, and looked at ways they could more confidently deal with his fiery temperament. I helped them learn how to communicate with Charlie in ways that left him feeling understood, even if he couldn't have what he wanted. Instead of "No, you can't have cookies for dinner" (*no* being a very triggering word for most children), I showed them how to respond in a less confrontational way to at least some his requests. "Cookies for dinner! Wouldn't that be fun! Should we try that for your next birthday?" And both Angie and Eric made more time to simply be present with their son so that he experienced the kind of closeness and connection he craved, and that would help him want to behave better and please his parents.

The Pitfalls of Parental Guilt

Things settled down with Angie and Eric. However, one issue still needed to be addressed: parental guilt and shame. As I shared suggestions with them about how to work with Charlie, they responded with comments like, "I should have known that" or "We've probably ruined our son forever." This didn't surprise me; I've worked with parents for decades and am well familiar with the tendency we have to beat up on ourselves when we fail to live up to our idealized standards. But I also know how harmful it is to allow that critical voice in our heads to govern our actions and feelings. Doing so not only hurts us, but in a roundabout way, it also puts pressure on our children to behave well so that we can feel good about ourselves and keep guilt and shame at bay.

> *Allowing that critical voice in our heads to govern our actions and feelings not only hurts us but also puts pressure on our children to behave well so that we can feel good about ourselves and keep guilt and shame at bay.*

This was something we had to work hard on. I shared with Eric and Angie my experience of taking on that judging voice in my own head — the one that ran a constant narrative about how I was doing in any given moment or interaction. One of the greatest investments I have ever made has been in learning to stand up to that voice — through therapy, EMDR (Eye Movement Desensitization and Reprocessing), meditation, and prayer. But it is a process, not something accomplished overnight or by simply setting an intention to be more positive.

One day I was in my closet and something slipped out of my hands. Right away, a voice in my head — an old voice — said, "Oh, brother! You're so clumsy!" *Instantly,* another voice chimed in with, "You don't get to talk to Susan that way!" I was thrilled to see that I had so internalized the work I'd been doing about being "good enough" that it had finally become part of me. While there are plenty of areas in which I still have much work to do, I have come to accept that I *will* make mistakes and lose my cool or my patience. As long as I can own those moments without letting my ego blame others or build justifications, I can allow my imperfections to be part of what makes me human.

Eric and Angie had their work cut out for them, but they were committed to learning how to stop allowing their harsh and critical inner voices to sabotage the healthier approaches they were taking with their son, giving themselves permission to have stumbles and setbacks. This part of the work was lovely — watching them relax and make peace with just doing their best. It was also inspiring to see them step more fully into a place of trusting that if they owned up to their shortcomings with Charlie, legitimized his feelings, and apologized as needed, they could stop turning every challenging parenting moment into a test of their spiritual mettle.

Our Own Growing Pains

Sometimes we hesitate to set limits with our kids because we're afraid of them; their tantrums are so scary or exhausting that we tiptoe around them to avoid triggering their upset. Other times we fear "killing their spirit" by depriving them of something they long for, perhaps remembering all too well how our parents dampened our own longings. And then there are times when we neglect to fully own the role of Captain because we are ambivalent about becoming a card-carrying grown-up.

Raising children catapults us into adulthood — or at least it offers us the opportunity to grow up, if we are ready and willing. But it can be something of a shock to realize just how responsible we need to be once we become parents.

One day, when my son was a baby and had just started eating regular meals, I fed him breakfast. I soon found myself thinking about what he would be having for lunch a few hours later. My first thought was to look around the room for the adult who would be taking care of things like this — the legitimately grown-up person who would be arranging regular breakfasts, lunches, and dinners. Before kids, my husband and I had been casual about mealtimes, throwing something together for ourselves at the last minute without a lot of thought or planning. As it dawned on me that I was going to be responsible for feeding this child *three meals a day for the next eighteen years,* I was gobsmacked!

Frankly, I didn't see myself as being that mature or together. But the truth was, when I had a baby, the decision to step all the way into adulthood had more or less been made for me. I had to catch up to the reality that *I was* the grown-up in the room and that I might as well step fully into that role. If we are actors on the stage of life, we might as well dress the part! Lo and behold, the greatest transformation of my life came about when I stepped further onto the stage of being a parent, discovering how great it is to grow up. And I didn't have to lose my playful or spontaneous side, as I had feared.

Children are born helpless and dependent. Mother Nature has instilled within parents a fierce urge to ensure their children's survival so that they can eventually negotiate life without their parents' protection. Kids naturally poke and prod against the limits we set to figure out where the end posts are in their world; otherwise they are at risk of venturing further and further off the map. Establishing boundaries helps us raise children who know how to handle disappointment and who are therefore strong, adaptable, and self-reliant.

> *Establishing boundaries helps us raise children who know how to handle disappointment and who are therefore strong, adaptable, and self-reliant.*

This is one of the grand prizes of parenting: seeing our children enter their adult lives capable of navigating life's inevitable ups and downs with confidence. That is when we know that the effort we made to grow up *ourselves*, while becoming loving stewards of our children, was worth all those growing pains — our children's *and* our own.

NOW IT'S YOUR TURN

Reflect on your childhood and how the way you were raised influences your ability to be the calm, confident Captain of the ship with your children.

1. Did your parents provide you with a healthy sense of what it is to be lovingly and clearly in charge?
2. How do you intentionally parent the way your parents did? How are you doing it differently?
3. Are there times when you are afraid to set limits with your children? What fuels your discomfort?
4. Describe any ideas or beliefs about growing up that might affect your willingness to be the adult in charge with your children.
5. If you often experience parenting guilt or shame, whose critical voice are you hearing in your head — that of a parent, teacher, coach, or someone else important to you as a child?
6. You may wish to do the exercise I did with Angie when I had her imagine the steel cable running all the way through her body, down into the earth. Holding this image clearly in your mind's eye, see if you can connect to a deeper strength within you that you can draw on in your interactions with your children, allowing you to be loving and kind and also steady and decisive.

MAKING IT PRACTICAL
Parenting with Presence in Real Life

Aren't children our equals?

QUESTION: As a spiritually minded person, I believe my children are very much my equals. I don't feel good about telling them what to do or crushing their spirits by setting limits that prevent them from following their hearts. How does that fit in with taking that authoritarian role you are suggesting?

SUGGESTION: For my birthday last year, my son's gift to me was a letter he had written about his childhood, thanking me for helping him grow into the man he is and is becoming. Throughout the letter, he recalled times when he was upset that I had said no to something he wanted to have or do. From his now-adult vantage point, he appreciated that I had been willing to hold my ground about what he now understood had not been in his best interests.

I can't describe how touched I was by this letter. I remember so well the times when I had to make an unpopular decision about something he wanted. If I was on the fence, I would invite him to respectfully make a case for why my no should be a yes. Sometimes he convinced me.

But when I was certain that no was going to have to be no, regardless of my son's anger or disappointment, I had to trust my instincts and keep my eye on the bigger picture, even when it meant letting go of those delicious smiles that I knew would be mine if I would just cave in.

I also recognized that my son — even when he was very small — was in every way my equal, on a soul level. (In fact, I frequently felt that *he* was the wiser one!) But I came to understand that children need someone to be a guiding, steady presence in their lives, even if it means not letting them do things they long to do — such as watching a movie that you know will give them nightmares or heading off to a party where there may be no parental supervision.

It is not easy to establish boundaries or to disappoint our kids, but perhaps like me you will come to see that it isn't about whether or not we are spiritual equals with our children; that goes without saying. It's about the fact that we have a duty and obligation to fully inhabit the grown-up role to the best of our ability. This might require being present with our uneasiness or discomfort about our children's anger toward us. But we shouldn't avoid those unpleasant feelings by abdicating the bigger need they have — for us to lovingly Captain the ship, steering them through storms as well as calm waters.

How do I not take it personally?

QUESTION: I find it extremely hard not to take it personally when my son misbehaves. This causes me to lose my footing and to react to him as if we were kids the same age, fighting it out on the playground after school. How do I remain the grown-up when he pushes my buttons?

SUGGESTION: Imagine yourself drifting along in a boat on a small lake, so relaxed that you begin to doze off. Suddenly another vessel slams into yours. Immediately you look for the person at its helm: How dare they ram their boat so carelessly into yours! What were they thinking? Your blood pressure begins to rise. How could they be so irresponsible!

As you rouse yourself and look for the offending skipper, you discover...there isn't one! The other boat must have come loose from the dock; it merely hit your boat because the currents caused it to drift there. With no one to blame, you immediately settle down, perhaps even looking for ways to secure the boat to yours so you can return it safely to shore.

What changed? Only your thoughts about the event. You realized that the boat ramming into yours was not piloted by someone intending you harm. *It wasn't personal after all.*

Choose to see your son's misbehavior as something other than a desire to offend or upset you. He may be tired or hungry or feeling shortchanged on attention. Or perhaps he is worried about something at school, or just out of sorts. Even if your son is deliberately yanking your chain, you can look beneath that motivation to see his behavior as a clumsy way of getting one of his needs met rather than something done maliciously.

One of the greatest gifts you can give yourself is allowing yourself to move through life without taking other people's behavior personally. A tornado doesn't deliberately rip apart a house; the house just happened to be in its path.

Go ahead and feel your frustration or disappointment, but spare yourself the suffering that comes when you believe your son means you harm. He is simply a boat adrift on the currents of his particular challenges. Address underlying causes of his misbehavior, but allow yourself the freedom to step back from taking it personally.

Can I be the Captain and still be fun?

QUESTION: Now that I am trying to Captain the ship, I feel I am in danger of becoming too strict. I used to be too loose and see now that it is better for my kids when I am more of a grown-up, but I don't want to turn into my mother, who was very serious and rigid. How can I be the Captain and still be a fun mom?

SUGGESTION: Kids are programmed to enjoy life. Thank goodness! Otherwise it would be a drab and dreary world, with everyone shuffling through the tasks on their to-do list, dutifully checking things off.

Remember, a pendulum swings from one extreme to the other

before it settles in the middle. It is common for it to take a little time to find your sweet spot when it comes to inhabiting the role as Captain of the ship without sacrificing the pleasure of enjoying life with your kids. In time you will become more comfortable setting limits when they are needed and appropriate, for example, when your kids want to play with matches or jump off the roof.

Eckhart Tolle tells a funny story of passing by a school that had just closed for summer vacation and had posted a big sign saying Be Safe! As he thought about this parting advice for students heading into their holidays, he laughed as he imagined the children returning from vacation at the start of the next school year. Eckhart said, "The most successful student will say, 'I was very, very safe over the holidays!'" Clearly, we want our kids to be careful *and* to explore the world and have fun.

My recommendation is this: When faced with a decision about whether to be flexible or firm with your children, pause and check in with yourself. Tune in to what your instincts tell you is the best course of action. Trust yourself.

Stand in your Captain role with confidence. You don't have to become your mother or come across like an army sergeant. If it's a good day to have ice cream for breakfast or announce a Stay in Your Pajamas All Day holiday, by all means, do that! The last thing I want is for parents to read my books and think they have to stop being goofy and lighthearted with their children. Don't forget: although ship captains exude confidence and know how to navigate stormy seas, they also take passengers for a twirl around the dance floor!

Children remind us to play, explore, and embrace life with great passion. While you have to be the grown-up in the room with your kids, don't ever let that put an end to filling your days with joy and fun.

CHAPTER 3

Throw Away
the Snapshot

*Reality is always kinder than the story
we tell ourselves about it.*

— Byron Katie

In an article in the *New York Times*, Eli Finkel offered some statistics on parents' quality of life after having children. "In a study published in the journal *Science*, people reported their emotional experiences during each of 16 activities over the course of the previous day: working, commuting, exercising, watching TV, eating, socializing and so on. They experienced more negative emotion when parenting than during any activity other than working. And they experienced more fatigue when parenting than during almost any other activity."

Grim, eh? What happened to the joys of parenthood — those sloppy kisses and joyful snuggles? While Finkel's piece was tough to read (he also quoted statistics reflecting the rise in clinical depression postparenting), it catalyzed a valuable conversation on my Facebook page and no doubt in homes across the country. It is only when we acknowledge our ambivalence about living the life in front of us — including child rearing — that we can find our way to embracing it.

As important as the article was, however, it left readers feeling

the weight of parenthood's unrelenting demands, with no light at
the end of the tunnel. Gazing ahead at eighteen years of sleepless-
ness, financial pressure, and diminished opportunities for sex is
not exactly enticing. While I would never suggest that depression
can simply be alleviated by a change of attitude, I believe that we
do ourselves no favors when we get locked into a negative out-
look about our circumstances. The truth is, raising kids *is* really
hard. And holding ourselves to a mythic standard of behavior
(*always patient, never cranky*) only fuels the depression Finkel was
talking about.

Parenting is thankless. "I want pasta with butter!" your child
demands, after you lovingly serve the organic, non-GMO stew
you've prepared for dinner. *It's messy.* Reach under the couch cushions, and who knows what decomposed food item you may find.
And it's exhausting. One mother told me that the greatest yearning
of her life was to have just one night of uninterrupted sleep.

As much as we aspire to move consciously through our parenting days, being responsible for the care and feeding of a child
doesn't erase our personhood or do away with our needs, moods,
or desires. We long to read for hours
or go to the bathroom without an audience. Naturally, we feel resentful at
times. There are going to be moments
when we lose our cool. Some days we
say things we wish we hadn't. That is
just the way it is. The trick isn't making the unpleasant experiences go away; it is making peace with them.

> The trick isn't making the
> unpleasant experiences
> go away; it is making
> peace with them.

Snapshot Child Syndrome

In *Parenting Without Power Struggles* I introduced the idea that we
have a hard time accepting our child not because of her problem-
atic behaviors but because we compare our real, 3-D child with

what I refer to as our Snapshot Child. The Snapshot Child says, "Sure, Mom!" when we ask her to take out the trash, while the real child lets out a groan. Our Snapshot Child says, "Thanks for reminding me!" when we ask him to start his homework, while the real one, in a trance in front of the TV, acts as though we don't exist. Our Snapshot Children lovingly get along with one another, sharing toys, hugs, and the last piece of cake. Their real counterparts — well, I think you get the picture.

As frustrating as it is when our child doesn't match up to who we would like him to be, we don't lose our cool because he is annoying or uncooperative. *We lose it because we think he shouldn't be annoying or uncooperative.* In other words, our difficulty in being fully present with whatever is going on with our children is fueled by the mismatch between our Snapshot Child — who exists only in our imagination — and the real flesh-and-blood one in front of us.

We move into Lawyer or Dictator mode not because our child "makes us" by misbehaving but because of a story — a "thought pill" we swallow — that negatively influences us. That upsetting story is then magnified by an army of inner attorneys who enthusiastically build a case to justify our grievances. If you find yourself thinking, *Jeffrey should help out around the house more cheerfully,* the team of lawyers in your head will eagerly provide evidence to support that belief, tossing in thoughts like, *He only cares about himself! I even have to nag him to pick up his towel off the bathroom floor!*

> *Our difficulty in being fully present with whatever is going on with our children is fueled by the mismatch between our Snapshot Child — who exists only in our imagination — and the real flesh-and-blood one in front of us.*

These stories and beliefs are only neutralized when we explore why our child's upsetting behavior makes its own kind of sense:

Jeffrey *should not* cheerfully help out around the house...*because he's a surly teen who is in the midst of heaping doses of peer problems.* Or Jeffrey *should* resist my demands that he help out...*because I come at him with irritation and sarcasm.*

When we view our child — and our life — from a wider perspective, we become better able to line up with reality instead of fighting it. If we need to make changes, we can respond from strength rather than reacting from desperation. Freeing ourselves from Snapshot Child syndrome means that we stop pushing away reality, acknowledging our resistance and allowing it to move through. As speaker and writer Byron Katie humorously says, "When you argue with reality, you lose. But only 100% of the time."

Just as we might struggle to accept the child we have — preferring the Snapshot Child to the real one — we may also struggle to accept the day to day realities of life with children, which may bear little resemblance to what we imagined it would be like. But therein lies a golden opportunity for stretching and growing.

For some, it's little things: We didn't imagine joining the PTA, but when we give it a try we discover an unexpected sense of camaraderie as we help out at a bake sale. Or maybe we're staunch pacifists and end up with a child who is fascinated with weapons. Lo and behold, we find ourselves throwing our heart and soul into a game of laser tag with our son and his buddies. When we remain inflexible instead of embracing reality, we run the risk of missing out on some terrific experiences.

Growing versus Grumbling

Nearly all of us face some mismatch between our idealized Snapshot Life and the reality we're living. For some, that snapshot is of a smiling mom and grinning dad surrounded by cheery kids and the family dog; reality might be an acrimonious divorce and an awful custody arrangement. For others, the snapshot might be of a posse of noisy children tumbling through the house. Reality could be a child with a disability, confined to a wheelchair. Another parent might have imagined a life of ease with vacations on the lake and private school for the kids. Economic downturns might instead have left the family in dire straits, crammed into a tiny apartment in a part of town they had assiduously avoided.

Seldom can we control our lives so effectively that we're spared unexpected plot twists. Human life brings with it countless opportunities to either resist or adapt. I've watched people in identical circumstances — serious illness, addiction, foreclosure — assume radically different attitudes about their life situations. Those who resist might suffer for years, angry at God, their former spouse, or their parents for "making them" deal with challenges they didn't sign up for. Others make peace with *what is* about their life, stepping into it with humility, acceptance, and appreciation for the smallest moments of brightness.

To grow from rather than grumbling about the mismatch between our idealized snapshots and our real life requires a lot of letting go. Hundreds of times a day we are offered the chance to make friends with a difficult moment rather than gritting our teeth as we endure it. It all comes down to *micro choices* — the tiny, moment-to-moment decisions we make about how to approach what is in front of us.

> *Hundreds of times a day we are offered the chance to make friends with a difficult moment rather than gritting our teeth as we endure it.*

Sometimes what's in front of us is baby poop dripping down our leg. My friend Elisha tells the story of being trapped on an overseas flight with his baby, who — to put it delicately — had a stomach issue. The flight would have been a *lot* easier if he and his wife had brought a few more packs of baby wipes. "I had to decide to just be present with what was happening in the moment, even while the contents of my son's smelly diaper leaked onto my one pair of clean pants. Funny enough, by not resisting what was happening, and by keeping my sense of humor, I found joy in the midst of that craziness! My wife and I were cracking up about the whole thing."

It's not hard to imagine an alternative version of that story along the lines of, "You won't believe what I had to endure on that flight! It was hell — the worst nine hours of my life!"

Time and again I am awed by the patience and grace I have witnessed as parents release their attachment to their Snapshot Life in favor of their actual one, even when faced with a tremendous hardship, such as a child with a serious illness. You might say, "Those parents have no choice," but they do; we all have a choice, every moment: Will I resist what's in front of me and live with bitterness and frustration, or will I align my body, mind, and spirit with the way things are, allowing myself to be at peace?

Of course, none of this means we should avoid doing whatever we can to create change when it is called for; I do not advocate passively letting life roll over us. But as the saying goes, *what you resist, persists*. While there's much to be said for having a vision board or a clear image of the life we want to create, we need to throw away the snapshot of what *should* be happening so that we can enjoy life with the children and circumstances in front of us, as they are.

Grieving for Your Old Life

After having led a serene, prechild life that included dance classes five days a week and a regular painting workshop, Sylvie felt adrift in a sea of demanding children. "I feel cut off from the very things that fed my soul," she confessed, "even though I love my kids with all my heart."

Like Angie and Eric, she was wracked with guilt over violating the "shoulds" of parenthood. "It's so much harder than I thought it would be. I know all the things I *should* feel — love, gratitude, delight — and I do feel those things some of the time. But my husband works very long hours, and I'm left on my own with an oppositional toddler and a bossy four-year-old. I feel like parts of me are dying. I find myself constantly checking my Facebook page to see what my friends are up to, trying to stay connected to a world outside of potty training and Barney. I feel terrible about how much I check out, removing myself emotionally when I'm with my children: *There, but not there.*"

Although Sylvie and I talked about the importance of making time to do things she loved, it was clear that just taking a few dance classes was not going to eliminate her resistance to the demands of her day-to-day life. I suspected that making peace with her current life was going to require her to grieve for the one she had had to let go of. Without doing that work, she would remain trapped in the in-between space — no longer living the life she inhabited before she had children but not fully available for the one that she was living now. Parenting from this partially present state is a recipe for child-rearing challenges; when kids sense our halfheartedness, they will do whatever is required to bring all of us into the room, even if it means tantrums, aggression, or defiance.

> *Parenting from a partially present state is a recipe for child-rearing challenges; when kids sense our halfheartedness, they will do whatever is required to bring all of us into the room, even if it means tantrums, aggression, or defiance.*

I told Sylvie, "The only way to neutralize your grievances about life with children is to grieve. And this will require turning *toward* your feelings, even if your instinct is to turn away from them." I invited Sylvie to quiet herself and tune in to the feelings underneath her resistance.

She told me, "I feel resentful and trapped. It's like I'm shut down or suffocating — and then I feel ashamed for feeling that way. After all, I wanted to have children; it isn't their fault that they have needs or can't give me the stimulation I get from the outside world."

I asked her to stay present with what she felt, without slipping into her head about what was going on. "What does that feeling remind you of, Sylvie? How is it familiar — that sense of being trapped or shut down?"

She stayed quiet for a few minutes, and then responded, "I know this feeling. It's like being a child who wanted more than anything to dance and be imaginative, and I wasn't allowed to do those things. Dance classes were out of the question in my family, and schoolwork took forever because I had an imaginative mind that didn't want to be bothered with boring assignments. I felt... trapped."

Exploring this led Sylvie to uncover a deep sadness over being raised by parents who were invested in trying to change who she was. Her parents were well-intentioned; as first-generation immigrants, they had made enormous sacrifices to raise their children in a country that offered opportunities for education and financial success they could only have dreamed of. But Sylvie was a very right-brained, creative child whose passion was in expressing herself through movement and art. Like all children, one of her greatest needs was to feel celebrated and cherished, *as is,* by her parents. She needed to know that she was a delight to them — that who she was was enough. "It is profoundly wounding to a youngster to feel that they are a disappointment to those they most love," I told her. "It's like being told that there's something wrong with your size-seven feet because they won't fit into the size-six shoes you're being told you should be able to wear.

"This wound — this longing to be free to express your unique qualities and interests — may be fueling some of the frustration you feel now with your children, since you have to tamp down your own interests to take care of your kids each day. It makes sense to me that you would feel resentful; it is, in fact, a big loss — letting go of the things that brought you a sense of joy and aliveness while taking on the mundane tasks of parenting."

In my sessions with Sylvie over the next few weeks I focused on helping her go deeper with her unresolved feelings about being forced to be who she wasn't in her early years. I encouraged her to acknowledge and allow space for her feelings, being present for the sensations in her body associated with them — heaviness, constriction, trembling — without checking out or slipping into a mental narrative about what she was experiencing.

As Sylvie stayed still and present to what she felt when she visited her sadness, the painful emotions began to lessen in intensity. She was surprised that by allowing herself to experience the feelings buried beneath her resistance and resentment, she could begin to move into a very kind and loving place — toward herself as well as her children. As this transformation happened, Sylvie softened; in fact, her whole demeanor seemed more relaxed.

A few weeks after we began, Sylvie shared this with me: "I don't quite know how it happened, but I'm finding myself much more patient with my kids — enjoying the little moments more. I'm less interested in switching on my phone to see what's going on in the 'real world' and more engaged with the things going on with my children. It's amazing how not hiding from my resistance is liberating me from it!"

When Anger Unleashes Anger

At times I am astonished by how quickly a client's long-repressed, unresolved feelings come to the surface when she is ready to face them. Cecilia was the mother of a five-year-old daughter and an eighteen-month-old son. Describing herself as gentle-natured, she scheduled a phone session with me because she became enraged when her daughter expressed anger. "As a child, I wasn't allowed to get angry. I want my daughter to know that she can express her upset, but when she does, I become furious."

I asked if a part of her felt that her daughter was breaking a rule — *kids shouldn't be angry* — when she got mad. She admitted that she did feel that way. When I suggested that it might also bring up feelings about the fact that while she had to bury her upsets as a child, her daughter was being permitted to express them, she agreed. It wasn't easy to reconcile the double standard she was facing — wanting it to be okay for her daughter to embrace unpleasant emotions that she herself had been required to suppress.

I invited her to simply sit with her anger, allowing it to be there without judging it. "Where in your body do you feel it? Describe the sensations to me."

"It's like a panic. I feel it in my stomach, and my feet feel like they want to move — like I want things to go faster. Like I want to escape." She went on to say that she also felt her face tighten, as though she was concentrating intensely — trying to make something happen.

"Don't get caught up in analyzing it. Just stay with what's going on and see if any other feelings are there, too, such as sadness, or fear, or longing." As soon as I said this, she said, "Yes, sadness. And longing…" She began sobbing; I could feel the depth of sorrow around whatever was being stirred up.

I remained quiet, letting her know that I was present with a few words here and there, while trying not to intrude on her process.

She described the longing as a black hole. "I can sense it's there but it is so big I can't reach it because I know I can't... have what it wants." As a child she told me she was not allowed to cry or to want things. And in spite of her parents and brothers expressing anger routinely, she was forbidden to do so. "I would be spanked and told to go to my room until I could be a 'good' girl again. I stayed there as long as I could, hot with anger but trying to numb it. I was a girl, and girls were expected to be quiet and good, and not make any trouble."

"It is so courageous of you, Cecilia, to stay with this grief and give it room. Thank you for being so brave." As her crying quieted, she told me that she almost never cries. I think she was surprised by how quickly those old feelings came to the surface when she gave them space.

In our conversation afterward, I explained that she was not the only one who would benefit from allowing these emotions to be experienced; her daughter would as well. "Anger is just the outward manifestation of hurt. It's likely that you are going to find yourself getting less angry with your daughter as you let the sadness have its say."

I also told her that by traveling this road, she would be better able to help her daughter move into her own sorrow when she becomes frustrated rather than lashing out in rage.

The next time we met, Cecilia told me that a new world had opened up for her as a result of that single breakthrough. She said she had no idea she could be less reactive. "Even my husband has noticed a calmness in my voice." But it was difficult to say no to her daughter, and she still got upset when her daughter defiantly said it to her. We talked about where that terror of standing her

ground had come from. I asked her to say no aloud a few times —
not as a plea, but as an announcement.

"I can feel it like a big pressure or energy in my belly, but I
can't get it out. It's like I'm choking on that feeling." I didn't rush
her. She started to cry. And then I heard her "No!" It was tentative but powerful, and behind it was a torrent of tears. As her no
got a little stronger, Cecilia cried and cried.

At the end of our session, she was much lighter. We laughed
about how perfect it was that she had such a feisty, strong-willed
daughter. I said, "Isn't it something, Cecilia, how the universe
works? It didn't send you a meek and mild child; it sent you a
strong one — one who can say, 'Here is what it sounds like to
stand up for yourself, Mommy!' so you could clean up these old
feelings around having needs, knowing it's okay to express them."

> *Our children often catalyze tremendous healing within us, if we turn difficult experiences with them into opportunities to give old feelings room to breathe.*

As discussed, our children often
catalyze tremendous healing within
us, if we turn difficult experiences
with them into opportunities to give
old feelings room to breathe. Such
was the case with Cecilia, whose willingness to heal painful wounds from
her past left me inspired by her courage.

In the previous two examples, both women's resistance to the
"what is" of their parenting lives had been strongly influenced
by unfinished business from their childhoods. I want to note that
while it is always good to look to the past for clues if we are experiencing significant emotional reactivity to our present-day lives,
I am not advocating that we blame mom and dad for all our woes,
or that we disregard the influence of current stressors. Tension in
a marriage, business-related difficulties, economic challenges, and
even hormonal imbalances can also contribute to resistance we
may feel toward our children or our life.

Relying on Our Kids to Make Us Feel Good

Resistance to the *what is* about our children also shows up when we view them as servants of our self-esteem, the means by which we feel better about ourselves. We may heap praise on our son when he scores the winning touchdown because we swell with pride from the admiring looks of other parents sitting in the bleachers. Or we might lavish attention on our daughter when she's polite to guests at the party, getting an ego boost when they remark on what a well-mannered little girl she is. There's nothing wrong with feeling pleasure when our child's talents or kind nature is recognized by others. But kids are exquisitely attuned to our feelings; they want our approval and they know the rules of the game for winning it. When we need them to be a particular way so that we can feel good, we create a wound because we are establishing conditions for our love and acceptance of them.

Accepting the *what is* about our children allows us to recognize them as separate people with their own strengths and challenges. It doesn't ask them to compensate for our insecurities. It doesn't make them responsible for our feelings. It lets us accept their shortcomings without fearing we will lose value in the eyes of those we believe are judging us based on our children's accomplishments. All this frees us from being ego driven, so that we can raise the children we have, as they are, with presence.

> *Accepting the* what is *about our children allows us to recognize them as separate people with their own strengths and challenges. It doesn't ask them to compensate for our insecurities. It doesn't make them responsible for our feelings.*

Dysfunctional Acceptance as a Form of Resistance

Acceptance also allows us to face rather than hide from any challenges our children may be struggling with. Lisa was the mother of fifteen-year-old Luke. She knew that her son's grades had been slipping, but she attributed this to ninth grade being a lot harder than middle school. When Luke came home from a party drunk, she scolded him but chose to believe his promise that it was his first and only time. "I hate the stuff, Mom."

When his friends showed up at their house furtively heading to Luke's room without making eye contact, she chalked it up to awkward teenage boy behavior. When she confronted her son about the smell of pot in his room, she believed him when he told her he didn't touch the stuff and it was probably that weird incense he was burning. Two of Luke's teachers emailed her to say that he was at risk of failing out of his first semester in their classes. She lectured him about trying harder, but nothing changed. Luke started sleeping till noon on weekends; she told herself that it was normal for his age. In other words, she resisted the *what is* about her son, refusing to acknowledge that he might be tumbling toward a substance problem, depression, or academic issues that needed attention.

Lisa wasn't a bad or negligent mom; she cared very much about her son and wanted him to have a good life. But she refused to line up with reality, choosing to see him as the innocent, carefree little boy he had once been. Her resistance to the *what is* about Luke manifested in the form of something I have heard Eckhart Tolle call *dysfunctional acceptance*. Without considering that his behaviors might be pointing to issues that needed to be addressed, she accepted at face value her son's explanations that he didn't like alcohol, didn't use pot, and that slipping grades and sleeping past noon were a normal teen phase. What seemed like acceptance was in reality a passive form of resistance, or hiding from the reality of her son's behavior — a dysfunctional acceptance of reality.

> What seemed like acceptance was in reality a passive form of resistance, or hiding from the reality of her son's behavior — a dysfunctional acceptance of reality.

It wasn't until Luke failed two of his classes that Lisa came to work with me. We found that he was indeed struggling with depression around social problems, long-buried feelings about his parents' divorce, and significant gaps in his math skills that left him in the dark about how to do the work. Luke had been trying to numb himself with pot, alcohol, and sleep. Lisa was shocked to find out how much trouble her son was in emotionally; she had chosen to look the other way, afraid of the guilt and sense of overwhelm she would have to face if her boy were genuinely in trouble.

Stretching beyond Ourselves

Rising to meet life as it is requires us to move through resistance in ways that might feel uncomfortable or even impossible. Every parent has stories about the ways they have had to stretch to accommodate the realities of parenting. Mine began the day I went into labor.

I am a strong and resourceful person, but in some areas I can be kind of wimpy. For instance, I'm not one to push myself when it comes to exercise. If I do manage to get past my excuses and procrastination, I may take a leisurely bike ride, or stroll along the treadmill for a few minutes. The truth is, I've never been very good about pushing through what I believe to be my physical limits.

So it was fairly soon after I went into labor, maybe after my fourth or fifth contraction, that I changed my mind about having a baby. Sure, I had been excited about the whole thing, but as things got serious, I decided that I wasn't up to it after all!

Twenty-seven hours later (with what would become two black eyes from having to push so vigorously that I burst blood vessels in my eyes) my nine-and-a-half-pound baby boy was born. I had toppled over the edge of what I thought myself capable of, and was now a proud mama lion who would do whatever it took to protect the child who had taken complete possession of my heart.

This is what parenting does; it invites us to stretch beyond ourselves, move through resistance, and tap into inner resources we didn't know we possessed. While every parent has endured challenges they might not have thought they could handle, parents often tell themselves that they *can't* be that Captain who knows how to navigate real storms. Once the going gets rough, they lose faith in their ability to deal with a child's rage over a divorce or to cope with the magnitude of problems resulting from the discovery that their teen has a real drinking problem. So they look the other way.

> *Parenting invites us to stretch beyond ourselves, move through resistance, and tap into inner resources we didn't know we possessed.*

But it is in the challenging moments that we get to move through resistance and strengthen our dedication to parenting with presence. Remember, muscle building cannot take place without tearing down muscle fibers — this is called hypertrophy. These microtears are what it takes to build muscle bulk. We grow ourselves up each time we listen without reacting when our child shares something that fills us with dread, teaching her that she does not have to hide the truth from us. We discover that we *can* respond sanely when she is hurting, rather than crumbling because of our own distress.

These are the moments that shape us not only as parents but as people. By throwing away the snapshot, bravely facing reality, feeling our feelings, and challenging the stories that suggest the grass is greener (or the child easier) in some other, imagined world, we can arrive fully at the life in front of us, with the very children we have been given.

NOW IT'S YOUR TURN

Quiet yourself for a few moments and focus on the feelings you experience when your child behaves in a way that upsets you. Perhaps your daughter is sassy, or your son shows little appreciation for the many things you do, making it hard to respond thoughtfully instead of reacting in anger.

Breathing deeply and steadily, sit with the anger. Don't try to analyze or talk yourself out of it, or make it more or less than it is. Just allow your feelings, without judging them as good or bad.

You may find that as you sit quietly with the anger, other feelings emerge, such as sadness, disappointment, loneliness, hurt, or a sense of being invisible or unimportant. If you notice other emotions, acknowledge them gently, the way a loving mother might offer comfort to a hurting child. Take your time.

Be present with any and all feelings, giving them space. The fury you initially associated with this upsetting behavior of your child's may mutate into something closer to sorrow or grief. You might be reminded of pain from your childhood, noticing that the anger you feel toward your child is fueled by these unfinished hurts. Let yourself feel whatever comes up, treating each emotion with respect and tenderness.

When you are ready, take a few moments to reorient yourself to the room, touching your heart in thanks for your effort and your courage to experience difficult feelings. If this exercise has generated noticeable distress, consider investing in professional counseling for additional support.

MAKING IT PRACTICAL
Parenting with Presence in Real Life

How do I accept my life, just as it is?

QUESTION: My marriage is ending, and I am having a tough time even dealing with ordinary problems with my kids, such as complaints about doing homework or having to brush their teeth. It is almost impossible for me to accept how my life is right now. I try to put my needs aside so I can be there for my children (who are also hurting), but I feel lost without the trappings of the life I always believed was so secure. I find myself drinking an extra glass of wine in the evenings just to make it through the day without feeling so depressed.

SUGGESTION: It is *so* very sad to say good-bye to a life you wish you still had and to face the uncertainty of what is to come. I cannot recommend strongly enough that you make time for whatever lifts your spirit and comforts your soul. If nothing else, when you model good self-care to your children, you teach them the importance of dealing with life's challenges rather than numbing ourselves to them.

Good therapy can be critically important when things are rough, as is the loving comfort of a tribe of faithful friends. Being tethered to a sense of peace inside can be a great help; perhaps yoga, meditation, or a mindfulness practice would appeal to you. And of course diet, sleep, exercise, and good self-care will be vital as you limp through these difficult days.

As much as we might try to do everything possible to prevent life from changing, sometimes we are forced to accept a new normal. I firmly believe that we come equipped with the resources to deal with whatever comes our way, but we have to find and then use them. By being truthful about the pain you are experiencing, you can address it; burying it will only make it surface in unhealthy behaviors. Being a parent doesn't mean being a martyr, denying your own needs, or repressing your emotions. Get the support you need to move through your grief, and despite what you might think today, you and your children will come through intact on the other side of this loss.

It may also help to identify the thoughts that influence you to define your current situation as grim. Pain is often generated by our beliefs and ideas about a circumstance rather than the situation itself. When your mind propels you into the future (with imagined loneliness or fear) or into the past (where there is longing or anger), you are likely to suffer. But if you bring yourself fully into the present moment — noticing your breath coming in and out, paying attention to the sensation of the air on your skin — you may discover that *in this moment*, you are fine. Identify the thoughts that cause you pain, and understand that you are not obligated to believe them.

If you are facing an actual problem right now, address it with focus and attention. But be vigilant about falling into a pattern of abandoning the present moment to be dragged into the past or future with stress-inducing thoughts. This is not meant to diminish the loss you are facing, but only to help alleviate the extra burden of unhappiness your mind may be generating.

How do I get the negotiations with my grandson to stop?

QUESTION: My husband and I have been raising our grandson for the last year and a half. I have tried to accept his defiant nature, but I am utterly worn out. *Everything* is a negotiation — wanting more time on his video games, insisting he'll do his chores "later," or refusing to take a shower because he's suddenly too tired. I understand that I do better when I stop wishing he would be a more easygoing child. But I want the battles and arguments to stop!

SUGGESTION: My previous book was all about dealing with power struggles, so I will touch on only a few points here. The first is this: When we *need* something from our children, we tend to come *at* them rather than alongside them, which activates their defiance. Kids smell desperation and they wisely understand that they are not meant to be responsible for our happiness. Outside of a close and loving attachment — the basis of genuine authority in our children's eyes — they are likely to push back when our interactions with them have the fragrance of neediness. It is human nature. I once heard someone say something very wise: *He who is most attached to a particular outcome has the least amount of power.*

Compassionately acknowledge your grandson's longing to postpone his chores or skip his shower with less investment in winning: "I know it's a thousand times more fun to play that game than to take a shower. And it must be even worse for me to show up, asking you to turn it off when you were almost ready to move to the next level." As simplistic as it may sound, validating his feelings will help.

I sometimes talk about relationships as having a pH value. In science, if a solution is too acidic, we don't bring it back to neutral by removing acid; we add alkaline, or a base, to restore pH balance. Similarly, when our relationships with others — spouses, children, grandchildren — are too *acidic*, we bring *them* back into balance by adding alkaline, which in my model means including more interactions that strengthen attachment.

The fact that your grandson is not being raised by either of his parents also suggests that he may have deeper issues — anger, grief, sadness — that influence his chronic resistance. A youngster who has been subjected to significant upheaval is familiar with feelings of powerlessness, prompting him to make extra efforts to exercise control in situations where he can. I trust that your grandson — and you — have had counseling and support to help him adjust to the change in his life circumstances, regardless of how much better it is for him to be in the loving care of you and your husband.

Make sure your grandson has help off-loading pent-up feelings of frustration and loss. And work on fortifying attachment, effectively changing the "pH" of the relationship so that he is less inclined to dig in his heels whenever you make a request. For more on attachment, please see chapter 9, or refer to *Parenting Without Power Struggles.*

In *The Art of War*, Sun Tzu says, "Supreme excellence consists of breaking the enemy's resistance without fighting." Avoid engaging in power struggles and arguments with your grandson. Instead, focus on building a connection that deepens his awareness that although you might *prefer* him to be more easygoing, you delight in him just as he is.

Is it okay that I don't always like my kids?

QUESTION: I feel a lot of shame saying this, but I have a dirty little secret. Sometimes I don't like my kids. I *love* them, but there are times when I just want to be left alone. In many ways I had to parent my mother, and I feel resentful that I always have to be "on" for my two children, even though I love them so much. I have meditated most of my life, and now it is hard to get even ten minutes alone. There are times when my kids are pounding on my bedroom door while I am trying to sit and meditate. Talk about not being very "spiritual" — they just want to be with me and I'm trying to tune them out!

SUGGESTION: Unless and until we look the truth squarely in the eye, we cannot change in ways that will ultimately serve us. Whatever we are experiencing — guilt, shame, exhaustion, awe, gratitude, joy — needs to be acknowledged for us to fully inhabit the complex person that we are. If you shy away from the moments when you aren't thrilled to be a parent, you will only push your resentment underground, where it will leak out in the form of impatience, sarcasm, or withdrawal.

Feel what you feel. It makes perfect sense that you would yearn for your prechild, unencumbered life. I can also remember times when I longed to be alone and meditate for a little while, only to hear that knock, knock, knocking on the door, accompanied by, "Momma! I *need* you!" And I recall hiding in the bathroom with a page-turner in the hopes that I might lose myself in the story the way I had enjoyed before becoming a mother. It is only by allowing ourselves to be present with whatever is going on that we can let feelings move through with grace.

We are, alas, simply human. We each bring to parenting the trials and travails of our own childhoods, paired with our unique temperament and nature. Some parents get lost in the joy and magic of raising children, never once glancing over their shoulder at the life they were living before their children arrived. But others step into the demands of parenting in fits and starts, doing their best to embrace the role but still haunted by a nagging uncertainty about whether they're cut out for the job.

And within all of us lives the small child who just wants to be on the receiving end of love, kindness, and support. When we include him or her in the care and presence we offer our children, we can generate deep healing for the wounded parts of ourselves.

My advice is to be immensely patient with yourself, allowing whatever you feel to bubble up and be known. You may find it valuable to work with a therapist to move through some of the old feelings of resentment that are weighing you down. And when family life gets too chaotic, *take a break!* It is far better to ask a friend or family member to help you out so that you can have some time alone than it is to vent your frustrations in ways that are hurtful to you or your kids. Some moms form supportive networks that allow them an overnight once every few months, just to have twenty-four hours to recharge and do whatever they feel like from one moment to the next. Just moving through a day without factoring in the needs of others can be highly rejuvenating.

CHAPTER 4

We Aren't Raising Children, We're Raising Adults

*If we are to teach real peace in this world,
and if we are to carry on a real war against war,
we shall have to begin with the children.*

— MAHATMA GANDHI

I'm sitting in my son's car with him, hashing out a misunderstanding. In a couple of days he'll be graduating from college. I have come to notice that these important milestones in his life often trigger some kind of argument between us, probably part of the unconscious process of easing him further out of the nest.

I am trying to explain why something he said pushed a button, and he's having trouble understanding why that particular thing would be an issue. Finally I say, "You cannot know why that triggers me because you have never visited the planet where I grew up." And he gets it. His face softens, his posture relaxes, and he offers a simple, "Wow."

In that moment, I understand that this is the essential ingredient in compassion: recognizing that even if we don't understand *why* someone reacts the way she does, her history and truth are as real for her as ours is for us.

> *This is the essential ingredient in compassion: recognizing that even if we don't understand why someone reacts the way she does, her history and truth are as real for her as ours is for us.*

At six-foot-five, my son, Ari, can seem imposing, but after even the briefest interaction it becomes clear that your heart is safe in his presence. As I consider how he came to be this way, I know that some of his nature is simply what he came with; I think kids are born with certain temperaments and that Ari arrived with a gentle spirit. But I also believe that many if not most kids arrive similarly amiable and undefended, and that we have the chance to help them make their way in the world with strength that doesn't overpower, compassion that soothes, and gentility that comforts.

I did my best to help my son understand that he had been born into great privilege simply by virtue of the fact that we never had to worry about having a home to live in or food on the table. We traveled to parts of the world where he could get to know people from disadvantaged backgrounds whose happiness was not predicated on wealth or possessions. We volunteered in our community so he could interact with people who might look him in the eye and let him know that his small effort to make their lives better meant something to them. I tried to do the things for our neighbors and friends that human beings do as members of the same tribe or passengers on the same boat, believing that paying lip service to good personhood or writing a check to a charity is not the same as showing up.

I made it a practice to notice the simple pleasures in our lives. The taste of lavender ice cream. Hearing a great joke. Lying in the grass at night, watching the stars. He began pointing things out to me: "Look at how the light is hitting the top of that mountain, Mommy. That's so pretty, isn't it?" "It sure is, honey. Thanks for making sure I didn't miss it!"

I tried to live in a way that helped him understand that carving out time for reflection, meditation, and looking out the window in stillness were elemental to staying authentic and true to myself.

But oh, my — how often I fell short of being the person I

wanted to be! Plenty of days saw me edgy, impatient, or lost in my own little world. I was by no means exemplary as a parent or person, slipping into Lawyer or Dictator mode more often than I'd care to admit. But I think I was *good enough* — an idea that frees us from attempting perfection, allowing us to simply do our best each day to inspire our children to do theirs. From the many late-night conversations Ari and I have had since he has stepped more fully into adulthood, I have discovered that my imperfections — coupled with acknowledgments and the fact that he continues to see me growing through my challenges — helped him develop a greater capacity to accept, forgive, and be imperfect himself.

What follows are some thoughts about what we can do to help our kids head into their adult lives with a head start at being conscious, present, joyful people — keeping in mind, of course, that they will eventually have to develop their own resources through the grit and tumble of their lives.

Picturing Our Children as Adults

When I was working on this book, I sat down to write in an outdoor courtyard with chairs and couches scattered around the shops. I spotted a comfy sofa, but when I sat down, I saw that it was blanketed in crumbs. The table beside it was littered with used coffee cups and crumpled napkins. What a mess! I thought about the people who had left their trash behind. Had their parents demonstrated by their actions that it was okay to leave messes for other people to deal with?

Many ingredients go into raising children to be conscious, resilient, and compassionate adults, including honesty, gratitude, responsibility — the list goes on. But we cannot simply teach these qualities through our words. Lecturing our kids about the importance of cleaning up after themselves or being kind to others means nothing if they watch us leave our cups and napkins behind

> *Bringing up children to become people we like and admire requires us to at least try to live the qualities we want them to embody.*

or hear us insult the waiter when she fails to take down our order correctly. Bringing up children to become people we like and admire requires us to at least *try* to live the qualities we want them to embody.

As I mentioned earlier, when I begin a phone coaching session with a client, I usually start by asking this question: "If you feel better at the end of this call, what would have happened? What insight, strategy, or unresolved conflict would we have addressed? Picture yourself relieved or grateful when our time together is over, and let's talk about your issue with your desired outcome in mind." I have found this to be an effective way to stay focused on what most needs to happen during our session.

In that spirit, I invite you to participate in an exercise to help infuse more intentionality and awareness into your daily interactions with your children. Think about the person you want your youngster to be when he is a full-fledged grown-up. Picture him at twenty-five, forty-five, or sixty-five years old. Imagine him surrounded by a loving cadre of friends, passionately pursuing a career, delighting in creative pursuits, and/or enjoying his role as a partner, spouse, or parent.

Consider the qualities your child possesses that make this rich, satisfying adult life within her reach. What attributes do you hope to instill within her that will ensure that she is excited to wake up every morning to greet a new day, equipped with the resilience she will need to survive life's disappointments?

If you need ideas, call to mind a person you greatly admire. It may be someone you know personally, or it could be a celebrated individual whose life exemplifies the characteristics you most value. This person can be living or deceased; he or she can even be a fictional character.

Make a list of the attributes embodied by this person. Perhaps you are touched by the fact that he treats all those he encounters with respect and thoughtfulness, regardless of their status or stature. Or maybe you find yourself inspired by his tenacity and willingness to push through obstacles. Maybe you love his energy — he brings a certain joie de vivre and lightness of spirit to everything he does. Or maybe, after interacting with this person, you always feel better about yourself, or about life in general. Use these ideas to help formulate a list of the traits you want to nurture that will help your child lead a wonderful life, long after she has flown the coop.

Essential Ingredients for Raising a Caring, Confident Child

How a child turns out is a function of an infinite number of variables — temperament; genetics; the parenting they received; their physical, emotional, and psychological health; their opportunities for education; sibling relationships; the network of supportive people in their tribe. In other words, there are no formulas that guarantee a youngster will become a conscious, confident, caring adult. Many factors are out of our control. But what follows are some of the ways that we *can* influence our children to become fulfilled and joyful grownups.

Keep in mind that even the most spiritually evolved people have been known to have had significant parenting problems, even while advising their followers on how to be more conscious and compassionate. There is no certificate or credential that ensures we'll show up as our most enlightened self every day or that we'll have kids who don't have problems. It's a day-by-day, hour-by-hour, minute-by-minute undertaking.

> *We each carry with us the influence of our own upbringing and the often unhealthy strategies we developed to protect our tender hearts.*

We each carry with us the influence

of our own upbringing and the often unhealthy strategies we developed to protect our tender hearts. Each of us has blind spots, regardless of how much personal work we have done. But it is never too late to grow and to change. And from what I have seen, nothing propels our evolution quite like raising children.

When we consider the characteristics that are important to instill in our children, we might say that we want them to be confident and respectful, resourceful and kind, resilient and responsible; the list is long, and we will discuss some of these traits in the pages that follow. But when most parents are asked what they want most for their children in preparation for their adulthood, they begin by saying, "I just want them to be happy." And here is where things get interesting. While there are many qualities that we can and should nurture in our children, there is one without which all other attributes become significantly less important: *we need to raise our children to know they are inherently worthy of love and happiness so that they will be able to absorb all the good that comes their way.*

> *We need to raise our children to know they are inherently worthy of love and happiness so that they will be able to absorb all the good that comes their way.*

We live in a time of unprecedented options for enjoyment and amusement: movies, music, video games, shopping malls, and of course diversions such as Facebook and other online worlds. The array of possibilities for "having fun" are only as limited as one's imagination.

And yet more teenagers and young adults die from suicide than from cancer, heart disease, AIDS, birth defects, stroke, pneumonia, influenza, and chronic lung disease *combined*. Every day, more than 5,400 suicide attempts are made by young people in grades seven through twelve. And the suicide rate for middle-aged Americans has risen sharply; according to the Centers for Disease

Control, from 1999 to 2010, the number of Americans ages thirty-five to sixty-four rose by nearly 30 percent.

Clearly, the dots aren't connecting. If we have greater-than-ever access to enjoyment, why aren't more of us feeling good? Unless an individual has created space *internally* to experience love and joy each day, she will move through life Teflon coated, unable to be touched by the gifts attempting to come her way. It's sort of like owning a helicopter but not having a landing pad for it. We need to help our children develop the capacity to *feel* they are worthy of love and happiness so that they will be capable of receiving it, in all its forms, when they grow up. Helping our children become accustomed to being loved and enjoying the sweetness of life is the greatest contribution we can make to their future happiness.

This is no small task. It is a lifelong journey to carve out room within ourselves to receive all the goodness of life. In his beautiful book *Perfect Love, Imperfect Relationships*, John Welwood writes of the core wound we each carry within our hearts — the lack of belief in our inherent lovability or our right to be seen and cherished as we are. "Not knowing, in our blood and bones, that we are truly loved or lovable undermines our capacity to give and receive love freely. This is the core wound that generates interpersonal conflict and a whole range of familiar relationship tangles. Difficulty trusting, fear of being misused or rejected, harboring jealousy and then vindictiveness, defensively stone-walling, having to argue and prove we're right, feeling easily hurt or offended and blaming others for our pain — these are just a few of the ways that our insecurity about being loved or lovable shows up."

So it is our challenge and opportunity to foster in our children

> *It is a lifelong journey to carve out room within ourselves to receive all the goodness of life.*

the living, breathing knowledge that they are worthy — as is — of being loved.

No parent remains consistently attuned to his child. We cannot always know what she needs or muster the energy to respond in a satisfying way. We get tired and impatient. We find ourselves distracted, stressed, or out of sorts. We may have an especially difficult child who wears us out with unreasonable demands. We are, alas, merely human, struggling with our own challenges and destined to fail in meeting our children's needs again and again.

> *It is our challenge and opportunity to foster in our children the living, breathing knowledge that they are worthy — as is — of being loved.*

Frankly, it wouldn't even be good for our kids if we were perfectly tuned in to them. Imagine the expectations they would bring to their later-in-life friendships or marriages if our children expected every desire or need to be fulfilled by others. Donald Winnicott, a British psychoanalyst, talked about the importance of simply being a "good enough mother" after realizing that babies and children actually benefited when their caregivers periodically failed to meet their needs, allowing them to develop resilience.

Starting in infancy, children do their best to make sense of the world in order to feel safe in it. They imagine their caregivers to be infallible so that they can trust in their ability to provide for and protect them. If a little one is being raised by a parent who rarely responds lovingly and appropriately to his physical or emotional needs, he will *not* think to himself, "Oh, Mommy is probably stressed from her long day at work. I know she loves me but she is just tired or distant because she has unresolved emotional issues."

Instead, the child concludes that Mommy isn't responding to his needs either because he is unworthy or because there is something inherently wrong with him. Thus begins a pattern of longing to be "met" by an attuned parent, handling disappointment when it doesn't happen by creating a belief structure that he, the child, doesn't *deserve* to have his needs met. He heads into adulthood guarded, less trusting, disconnected from his heart, and therefore less available to receive all of life's goodness.

Like the child with his nose pressed against the window of the candy shop, this kind of person may yearn for all the delectable things inside, believing at his core that they are meant to be enjoyed by others but not him. He might blame his wife, his boss, or his unfair life circumstances for not delivering what he longs to have, when in fact even if everything he dreamed of landed in his lap, he would still be unable to enjoy it.

Our kids deserve to know that even if we can't always meet their needs or offer them the validation they long for, they are still wholly lovable and uniquely brilliant just as they are. This instills in them the consciousness that they *are* worthy of being loved and happy, positioning them to receive the wonderful things life has in store for them rather than conditioning them to push those things away.

> *Our kids deserve to know that even if we can't always meet their needs or offer them the validation they long for, they are still wholly lovable and uniquely brilliant just as they are.*

What can we do? It's not complicated. When we aren't able to be there for our child in the way she wants, we can minimize the harm by simply acknowledging her disappointment. "You were really hoping I could spend time with you, and here I am again with the baby." "I am sorry I was cranky — I had a tough day at work today, and I guess I got really tired — it was not your fault." "It's hard having to go to bed when we were having so much fun together." This helps prevent the possibility that she will come away from disappointment believing she is unworthy of attention because of an inherent defect.

When we engage with our children *with presence* as a *good-enough* parent, they come to know that they are worthy of love, kindness, and the infinite blessings of life. It is not a matter of telling our kids how terrific they are, nor is it about becoming a paragon of parental virtue — a robotic Stepford parent who never loses her temper or wishes she could escape the chaos and craziness of life with kids. Rather, it is through the overall quality of our engagement with our children that they come to understand how precious they are. In this way, they come to develop what Thupten Jinpa, longtime English translator of His Holiness the Dalai Lama describes as "self-liking, or an easy-going peace" with themselves.

> When we engage with our children with presence as a good-enough parent, they come to know that they are worthy of love, kindness, and the infinite blessings of life.

The following chapters offer suggestions on ways that we can support our children's success in life, in every meaning of the word.

NOW IT'S YOUR TURN

Think about the qualities you want to encourage in your children (respect, honesty, accountability and so on).

Which of these qualities would you say you exemplify? In other words, which characteristics are predictable elements of how you lead your life?

Which of these qualities would you like to develop in yourself while fostering them in your children? In other words, which attributes do you aspire to weave into your life, even if they don't yet come naturally to you?

CHAPTER 5

Modeling Self-Love
and Awareness

Be kind whenever possible. It is always possible.
— Tenzin Gyatso, the Fourteenth Dalai Lama

When I ask parents what trait they most want to cultivate in their children, one of the responses I hear most frequently is *respect*. We know that treating others respectfully is essential to getting along in life. But we sometimes forget that to truly respect another person, we must first respect ourselves. It may sound obvious and perhaps even a little clichéd, but I believe that *genuine* self-respect (as opposed to ego-driven, foot-stomping, "I demand to be listened to!" behavior) is not easy to develop. It starts by enjoying our own company and includes caring for ourselves with kindness, trusting our instincts, and pursuing the things that give our life meaning. Only then are we able to authentically respect others in how we communicate, empathize, handle disagreements, and honor our agreements.

Living in the 3-D World

In a series of experiments conducted in 2014 by Timothy Wilson from the University of Virginia, college students were invited to sit in a room alone with their thoughts and without distractions. They were simply being asked to sit for between six and fifteen minutes without falling asleep. In one of these experiments, participants were given a mild shock — a light, static electricity jolt — before they entered the room where they would be doing their quiet sitting. After they received the shock, nearly every subject reported that it was so unpleasant they would agree to pay five dollars to avoid receiving it again.

However, in one of these studies, after having once endured the shock and subsequent six to fifteen minutes of time sitting alone in the room, 67 percent of the men and 25 percent of the women actually requested a second shock if it would excuse them from having to complete the full "thinking period." They preferred being zapped to the prospect of sitting for six to fifteen minutes alone with themselves. My goodness!

A few years ago I was driving a friend's three-year-old home in their family's SUV. When the car started, the video she had been watching resumed playing. I was surprised but said nothing. In my day (which makes me sound much older than I am), the idea that my son would watch a screen *while we drove* would have been absurd. Why would you want to look at a screen when there is so much to see out the window? But when this little girl's show ended, she immediately started crying. "Put on another one! I want to see another one!" I suggested that she might have fun looking out the window at the cars or the people going by. She was having none of it. Poor thing — at three, she had already been conditioned to need some kind of electronic stimulation to tolerate car rides.

Most parents confess that if they left it up to them, their kids would never turn their devices off. The advent of smartphones, computers, tablets, and "phablets" has left parents swimming in uncertainty over how much time their kids should spend with these devices in order to stay current with the modern world, without crossing the line into oversaturation. (Frankly, it has left parents reeling over how much *they* should be on their devices as well!)

Children need to play. They need the tactile touch of gooey finger paint rather than the sanitary experience of brushing their fingers across a touch pad to make color magically appear on a screen. They need to dig in the dirt, and get dirty. They need to splash in water and get wet. They need to make music and climb trees. They need to wander aimlessly from room to room without an organized activity to occupy them.

> *Children need to play. They need the tactile touch of gooey finger paint rather than the sanitary experience of brushing their fingers across a touch pad to make color magically appear on a screen. They need to dig in the dirt, and get dirty. They need to splash in water and get wet.*

The Forest schools in Scandinavia were built on the premise that children learn best by doing and by being outdoors. Kindergarteners spend their entire two and a half hours outside. Unless temperatures drop below 20 degrees, I'm told that even children attending the Forest school in the Arctic Circle are outside playing and learning — with miner's lamps on their heads!

A child who is plugged into an electronic babysitter whenever he complains that "there's nothing to do" becomes an adult who is incapable of being alone with his thoughts for more than fifteen minutes. In *The Mindful Brain*, Dr. Daniel Siegel says,

> The busy lives people lead in the technologically driven culture that consumes our attention often produce a multitasking frenzy of activity that leaves people constantly doing, with no space to breathe and just be. The adaptations to such a way of life often leave youth accustomed to high levels of stimulus-bound attention, flitting from one activity to another, with little time for self-reflection

or interpersonal connection of the direct, face-to-face sort that the brain needs for proper development. Little today in our hectic lives provides for opportunities to attune with one another.

This doesn't mean that kids should be prevented from watching TV or using computers. I am not advocating that we raise a generation of Luddites. The digital era has brought countless benefits into our lives. But given the limitless stimulation offered by electronic devices and the potential exposure to things that are entirely inappropriate, it is crucial that we engage our children early in conversations about using these gadgets so that as they move into the independence of adolescence and are less under our influence, they will be able to make intelligent choices. Like us, they will have to figure out how to balance their plugged-in life with their unplugged one. I will be sharing more suggestions for how to manage that challenging balancing act as we proceed.

Hitting the Off Switch

One day a mother and her twelve-year-old son were having a heated argument in my office about time spent on his devices. Elena complained that her son refused to get off the iPad unless she forced him to by threatening to take it away altogether. "He ignores his chores, procrastinates on homework, and wouldn't dream of going outside to play." She said the hardest time was when she was making dinner; Christopher typically got on one device or another while she was occupied in the kitchen and therefore less able to follow through with limits. Chris maintained that his mom was far too strict. "She's so much meaner than my friends' parents. They get to be on the iPad for hours!" I let him air his complaints so that he would be receptive to my input. "There's nothing to do that's fun at my house! And I get my homework done. I don't see why she can't let me play my games. I'm not bothering anybody!"

Instead of trying to force Chris to embrace the merits of old-fashioned play or convince him that until recently kids managed to enjoy their childhoods quite nicely without the existence of iPads or computers, I invited the two of them to do a visualization with me. "Close your eyes, and imagine that the three of us are in the exact same spot we're sitting in now, but it's ten thousand years ago. There are no buildings or furniture, no cars or electricity. Chris, imagine your mom working around the fire with the other women of the tribe, preparing dinner — maybe grinding seeds or dropping in some of the herbs that you gathered earlier with her. Now, Christopher, I want you to picture yourself in that setting, a young man of the tribe. What are you doing? See yourself there and picture what you're doing while you wait for the meal." I let him have some quiet time and then invited them both to open their eyes.

"So, Chris, what were you up to, back when there weren't any devices?" He said he had pictured himself running around with the other boys, building things, and climbing trees. Elena chimed in, offering that she had imagined him helping the men — who were not that much older than he was — preparing weapons for their next hunt or building a hut.

He smiled as we talked about life back then. "I wish I could live like that now! It was cool!" I was reminded of how challenging it actually *is* for kids these days, now that opportunities to explore the great outdoors or spend time out in the wild are so rare.

I said as much to Elena, inviting her to see her son's situation from his vantage point. "Life is different now. It's hard to resist the temptation to switch on a device when you can't roam the great outdoors." His mom nodded, acknowledging the many restrictions of their daily life — including living on a busy city street where it was unsafe to wander too far. "Chris, would you be willing to make a list of at least ten fun things you could do that didn't require electricity?" He was surprised by how quickly he was able to come up with ideas, with his mom enthusiastically tossing in possibilities. Elena agreed to help him implement some of the activities on his list, such as getting materials for soap carving or building a small fort in their backyard. The session ended with Chris and his mom feeling more like allies than adversaries. This exercise didn't eradicate Christopher's love affair with his iPad and video games, but it did help him find something else to do when his mother asked him to turn things off. This issue will probably continue to be a challenge, because, as he said, most of Christopher's friends have fewer restrictions, and he wants to be part of their online culture. But once Elena was clear, and invested a little time into providing some interesting alternatives, the negotiations tapered off.

Steve Jobs's Kids and the iPad

Many parents justify giving their kids carte blanche when it comes to digital devices because they believe that not doing so will cause their children to fall behind in a competitive world where the tech savvy prevail. In his article "Steve Jobs Was a Low-Tech Parent," Nick Bilton began with a question he posed to Mr. Jobs as the first tablets were being marketed. "So, your kids must love the iPad?" Jobs's response? "They haven't used it.... We limit how much technology our kids use at home." Bilton spoke with Walter Isaacson, author of *Steve Jobs*, who spent a lot of time at their home and said, "Every evening Steve made a point of having dinner at the big long table in their kitchen, discussing books and history and a variety of things. No one ever pulled out an iPad or computer."

Chris Anderson, former editor of *Wired* and chief executive of 3D Robotics, puts time limits as well as parental controls on all the devices in his family's home. "My kids accuse me and my wife of being fascists and overly concerned about tech, and they say that none of their friends have the same rules," he said of his five children, ages six to seventeen. "That's because we have seen the dangers of technology firsthand. I've seen it in myself. I don't want to see that happen to my kids." Rule number one? "There are no screens in the bedroom. Period. Ever."

When our guidelines are clear, children adapt. They may push and prod to have more of what they want, but once the power is switched off, they will find something fun to do, just as children have done since time immemorial.

When I was in West Africa several years ago, I was curious about how people there were using social media. I asked a number of sixteen- to twenty-four-year-olds if they would ever consider being on their computers, perhaps on Facebook, at the same time that their friend was in the room, visiting with them. They always laughed at this idea. "That's very funny! Why would I want to be on my computer talking to my friend if she is here with me?" But in many homes, that is exactly how kids hang out with one another — texting, chatting, taking selfies, or showing one another posts and videos on the screens in front of them instead of just enjoying each other's company.

Comedian Louis C. K. did a hilarious piece on our growing obsession with our devices, joking about how parents no longer actually watch their children at their musical recital but instead solemnly hold their cell phones out in front of their faces to video the performance so they can post the footage on Facebook or YouTube where, truth be told, no one else cares to watch it.

When we fail to set limits because we're afraid of our children's meltdowns or we're feeling guilty about how preoccupied we've been with our obligations, we effectively toss our kids into the black hole of the digital world. Children need to live in the 3-D world; it is our responsibility to ensure that they do.

There are no hard-and-fast guidelines for digital use. There may be days when you're under the weather and your kids watch back-to-back episodes of *SpongeBob*. You may let them play "educational games" on your iPad while you indulge in a long bath. The problems begin when we abandon our instincts and parent out of fear or guilt.

Leading by Example

There is, of course, another piece we must discuss when talking about raising children who are comfortable being with themselves. *We have to show them what that looks like.* Most of us move at a frenetic pace throughout our day, hardly stopping to sit for a meal, let alone to gaze out the window or daydream. The beeps, the tweets, the pings, the rings — we have developed Pavlovian responses to the alerts our devices deliver, often dropping whatever we were doing (including, perhaps, giving our child a few minutes of undivided attention) as soon as one of those bells goes off.

How can we ask our children to be more engaged with the 3-D world or to watch the clouds go by if we aren't?

In *The Joy Diet*, Martha Beck talks about stopping our outward momentum for at least fifteen minutes a day. "[The problem is that] perpetually doing, without ever tuning in to the center of our being, is the equivalent of fueling a mighty ship by tossing all its navigational equipment into the furnace." She goes on to say, "The voice of your true self is so small and still that virtually any distraction can drown it out, especially if you're just beginning to hear it. You simply cannot develop the skill of listening without carving out and vigorously defending chunks of time during which to do nothing." (For an exercise on Doing Nothing, please see chapter 11.)

Enjoying our own company, disengaged from external stimuli, is essential to our happiness. If we fail to help our children learn how to be alone, they will always be lonely. It is only when we are truly comfortable in our own skin that we can attract and sustain healthy relationships.

> *If we fail to help our children learn how to be alone, they will always be lonely.*

Many people pair up with a romantic partner who they know in their heart of hearts isn't a good fit, simply because they are so uncomfortable being with themselves. But just having another person around doesn't quell loneliness; many of my married clients often express great despair over their sense of isolation, even when they have a wife or husband next to them in bed each night. Chasing after someone to fill the empty places in our hearts only creates different problems; it does not solve them.

If you want your children to be happy without needing something or someone to drown out the noise of their discontent, unplug the electronics at your house and do nothing now and again. See what happens as you become reacquainted with yourselves, each other, and the simple, satisfying ways that human beings enjoyed life long before landing in the digital world.

Appreciating Our Body, Imperfections and All

I talk to my body a lot. Sometimes out loud.

I don't usually share this fact with people (which makes it kind of interesting that I'm putting it into a book that I hope will be widely read). But the fact is, I place a lot of stock in having loving conversations with my body and its many miraculous parts and have decided that it is an idea worth sharing.

"Thank you stomach, for digesting that meal so nicely."

"Thanks, eyes — what a great job you did in letting me see the colors of those flowers today!" "Thank you, heart, for beating so reliably and keeping my circulation going. You're amazing!" "Thank you, legs, for ferrying me around so nicely...thank you, ears, thank you, liver...bones...knees...teeth..." This love fest with my body can go on for quite a while. I nearly always find that my heart is soft and melty by the end.

Almost all of us take our body for granted until it breaks down, and then we can be quite mean to it, complaining about its failure to do what we want. And then there are the features we loathe; lips we wish were fuller, the nose we wish were daintier. If you consider how relentlessly critical we are of our human container and how it still plods on thanklessly, it really is a wonder that our physical systems work at all. If we treated employees with the sort of disdain we so frequently show our body, they would walk off the job. And yet our bodies carry on doing their duties as best they can.

Years ago I took a workshop during which we were given a paper bag with two holes cut out for the eyes. We were instructed to take it up to our hotel room, remove all our clothes, and stand in front of a mirror with the bag over our head. The assignment was to look through the holes at every inch of our bodies, noting the commentary in our head as we viewed ourselves. It sounded very weird.

But it was a life-changing experience. I began by focusing on all the things I *didn't* like — the parts that were too big or too small, too soft or too wrinkled. As I eased into the exercise, however, I fell into a place that was almost holy. I moved from noticing how harshly I judged each part of my body to realizing what a gift it had been to receive it and how perfect it was, exactly as it was.

I saw the pooch in my belly as evidence of the blessing of motherhood. I recalled how my slightly wobbly knees had rallied through achiness to get me to the tops of mountains. I reflected on how my arms had cradled my loved ones. By the time I got to my feet I was overcome with thankfulness...and remorse. Those feet! They had tirelessly ferried me through life for decades, almost never receiving a word of thanks. I felt waves of appreciation for the vessel I had been given, a gift extraordinaire — and one I had endlessly criticized for not being somehow different, or better.

We reassembled after the exercise to write letters to our bodies, then listened as people shared expressions of contrition, gratitude, and shame toward the miraculous heart-and-soul containers each of us had been allowed to inhabit. The room was pin-drop silent. Between racking sobs, a man in a wheelchair described the horrible things he had said to his body for years, angry at all the ways he had believed it had failed him. An overweight woman spoke of the unhealthy habits she had inflicted on her body to keep love and lovers at bay. The room filled with a quiet hum of gratitude. It was just a weekend workshop exercise, but it awakened something in me that thankfully remained.

> *When your children see you acknowledging the wonderfulness of your body instead of complaining about what you don't like about it, they will be far more likely to regard their own bodies — warts and all — with respect, care, and appreciation.*

Thank your parts for serving you and allowing you to dance and sing and eat and see and smell and touch and climb. When your children see you acknowledging the wonderfulness of your body instead of complaining about what you don't like about it, they will be far more likely to regard their own bodies — warts and all — with respect, care, and appreciation.

Enlisting Your Tribe

From time to time a weary mother plops down on the couch in my office looking like something the cat dragged in. I soon discover that she has been running on fumes. She sleeps five hours a night if she's lucky, and her slumber is usually interrupted by a child visitor climbing into her bed and thrashing about, making peaceful sleep something she can only dream about. For sustenance, she nibbles the remains of her children's unfinished meals as she hustles around the kitchen, never sitting down for a proper meal. She laughs when I ask about the last time she read a book and can't remember what it feels like to engage in a meaningful adult conversation with anyone other than her partner, with whom she discusses...the kids.

I have been known to send this type of client away after a few minutes in my office, asking her to follow some instructions for at least one week, after which she is free to come back for a session. "I would like you to drink water the minute you notice you feel thirsty, eat something nutritious within a few minutes of realizing you are hungry (while sitting down), pee as soon as you feel the urge (many have gotten used to holding it until it's unbearable), and rest with your feet up and your eyes closed — even for three minutes — when you feel tired."

My client usually thinks I'm joking and laughs a little nervously. She quickly finds out that I'm serious. I tell her, "Until you begin taking care of yourself, whatever work we do together with regard to your children or family is irrelevant."

Now, mind you, I don't do this very often; while most of the parents I work with fall short in some way when it comes to self-care, what I have described is extreme. But when I have parents

— yes, they are usually women — who have thoroughly abandoned any sense of loving care toward their body and spirit, I
send them home. (In fact, at times I tell them to just go and have
a rest in their car since someone is looking after their kids for at
least as long as they were meant to be in session with me!) I want
them to understand that unless they shift their attitude and behavior toward meeting their own most basic needs, they will not be
up to the task of being the Captain of the ship with their children.

It is simply impossible to parent in ones or twos and not feel
frayed at the edges, if not outright exhausted. We are not supposed to raise kids on our own; we are meant to do it as part of a
tribe. In her beautiful essay "I Miss the Village," Bunmi Laditan
writes,

> When one of us was feeling sick or needed extra rest from
> a long night up with a child, we'd swoop in and tend to
> your children as we would our own for as long as nec-
> essary — no need to even ask. You would drift off to a
> healing sleep with full confidence. We'd want you to be
> well because we'd know that we're only as strong as our
> weakest member — and not only that, we'd love you, not
> with the sappy love of greeting cards, but with an appre-
> ciative love that has full knowledge of how your colors
> add to our patchwork....I miss that village of mothers
> that I've never had. The one we traded for homes that,
> despite being a stone's throw, feel miles apart from each
> other. The one we traded for locked front doors, blinking
> devices and afternoons alone on the floor playing one-
> on-one with our little ones.

Parents — build yourselves a tribe. Not only is it essential to
your sanity and health, but it is an essential ingredient for raising

> *It is virtually impossible for one or two parents to raise a child alone. We require propping up, and time to ourselves.*

a confident, conscious, caring adult. It is virtually impossible for one or two parents to raise a child alone. We require propping up, and time to ourselves. And when we have challenging children, it is vital that we receive extra guidance, support, and simply — a break. A woman I know who has cancer said, "If you're there for my kids, you're there for me." Please, expand your network.

In addition to the support and camaraderie that our tribe can provide us as parents, it is also important that our children develop healthy attachments with other trustworthy adults. In one of the tribes we visited in Tanzania, little ones wanting comfort or a cuddle simply grabbed onto the leg of the nearest mother. The laughter among the women was easy and relaxed. Kids wandered, big and small mixing together. In New Zealand I spent time at a tiny country school, where the children played barefooted soccer — five-year-olds and thirteen-year-olds happily tumbling around together. "They have to get along," the headmaster told me. "They're all they've each got."

Children who feel they are part of a community grow up feeling anchored. I urge you to look around for a group of like-minded, like-hearted parents with kids reasonably close in age to your own. Plan ways to spend more time together, as friends and partners in raising children, offering one another support, respite, and time to recharge.

Appreciating Ourselves

We cannot talk about self-care without looking at the ways we talk to ourselves in the privacy of our own thoughts. As a therapist, I am privy to an unfiltered glimpse at people's self-talk, and let me tell you, it isn't pretty. "You can't do anything right!" "You're so fat!" "Why would anyone love you?" I often ask my clients how they would react if a friend spoke to them the way they sometimes speak to themselves. "How long would you let that person remain in your life if they said things to you like you say to yourself?" Usually, the answer is instantaneous. "If another person spoke to me like that, I'd want nothing to do with them!" And yet we are ruthlessly unkind to ourselves.

I frequently do online classes, and in the first session I often set the stage for the work we're going to be doing together, reminding parents on the call that as they learn new approaches, they may be tempted to be self-critical if they fail to implement a new idea, or resort to yelling or threatening. I tell my students, "There's nothing wrong with feeling uncomfortable when we say or do things that don't reflect the parent we aspire to be. If you put your hand on a hot stove, you want it to hurt. So there's value in a momentary, 'Oof! I didn't like doing that.' Where we get into trouble is when we then beat ourselves up, perhaps replicating the shaming voice of a parent or a teacher in our head. That is in fact quite harmful because when we feel shame, we become defensive and often lash out even more at our kids, repeating a vicious cycle."

I received this email in the midst of a three-part online class I taught for Glennon Melton's Momastery tribe.

The day after watching part two of the webinar, my husband and I received a letter in the mail from the city saying the weeds in our front yard were too tall and we needed to cut them. We bought the house in this shape a few years back with the hopes of fixing the front yard, but I was seven months pregnant and we had a two-year-old when we moved in. However, it has always bothered me. We live in a neighborhood of perfect front yards and throughout my life my dad has always emphasized appearances, especially in homes. I have always had his voice in my head telling me how horrible my yard looked, and sometimes I even had his real voice telling me how horrible my yard looked.

Well, after opening the letter I went into full panic mode. I ended up on the floor in my kitchen with my head between my knees because I was on the verge of tears and a total panic attack. And then I took everything we have been learning through this webinar and I applied it to myself.

I started saying out loud the stories I was saying in my head: "My neighbors must hate me," "I knew they were shunning us — they must have complained," "They must think I'm so lazy.... Well, I am so lazy — just look at my front yard" "If my dad found out he would say, 'I told you so.'"

After hearing the stories I was telling myself, I decided to tell the truth out loud, "I'm a really busy mom of two young kids." "My husband and I both work full-time." "My kids are a higher priority right now, and I don't have enough time for them as it is." And then I gave myself a pat on the back and burst into tears.

All this is to say *thank you*! I truly don't believe I understood the power of those voices in my head. I was destroying myself as a person and as a mother. For as long as I can remember, I have lacked self-love and self-confidence because the voice in my head was so clear and so negative. And now that I have the tools to change that, I am so excited!

As I lay in my four-year-old daughter's bed last night, she showered me with kisses as I told her all the reasons

I loved her (not accomplishment based). I realized how much her bedtime has changed. Thank you both for teaching me to embrace my "messy, beautiful life."

I read this woman's email and sat quietly for a long time, touched and inspired. Her story was my story, and your story, and the story of everyone who is walking a path of healing. I am simply awed by the beauty of the human spirit.

Not long ago I interviewed Thupten Jinpa, the primary translator for the Dalai Lama. I asked Jinpa if His Holiness ever spoke about parenting. His reply astonished me. "His Holiness, he's one of the most compassionate people I've ever met. He said, 'When I look at the parenting experience I sometimes wonder — if I were a parent, would I have that kind of patience?'"

My! If the Dalai Lama isn't sure *he* would have enough patience to parent, surely we can all relax a little bit about our shortcomings! It is only when we accept ourselves with compassion, warts and all, that we can further our growth through the stumbles and tumbles of raising children.

> *If the Dalai Lama isn't sure he would have enough patience to parent, surely we can all relax a little bit about our shortcomings!*

I think one of the greatest shifts I have made, both as a mother and as someone doing her best to keep growing, was to make peace with my imperfections. Until we accept, appreciate, and love all of ourselves, as is — body, mind, and spirit — we simply cannot ask others to treat us well. If we want our children to move into adulthood with confidence and a sense of self-love, we must show them what that looks like.

I've discussed some of the ways we can help our children know themselves to be worthy of love and respect. The final piece is to encourage them to choose their friends wisely, pruning out those who treat them disrespectfully or unkindly.

Maintaining Healthy Boundaries in Relationships

This morning I turned on the tap to run some hot water into the bathroom sink. After what I thought was plenty of time for it to get nice and hot, I felt the temperature. Lukewarm. I let it run a little longer and checked again. Still not hot. Ran it even longer. What was the problem? I finally figured out that I had unintentionally turned on both faucets — the cold along with the hot. As long as there was cold in the mix, that water was *never* going to get hot.

It made me think of my relationships and how difficult it has been to accept the *what is* about people in my life so that I could adjust my expectations accordingly. Just as that water was never going to get hot because there was cold in the mix, some people are never going to be able to show up in the ways we wish, for reasons we may never understand. Something else is in the mix; the cold is on.

When we love someone who is not good for us, it can be difficult to accept that we may not be able to continue the relationship. Perhaps she is dishonest. Or he may be abusive. In some cases, we can feel tremendous love for someone who is quite toxic for us, either intentionally or because of his own woundedness.

Many times I have watched children chase after friends who throw them a crumb now and then but who generally treat them terribly. In her book *Odd Girl Out*, Rachel Simmons talks about the lifelong impact of girlhood cruelty on women in their forties and beyond. In my own life, I have anguished over people I have loved who I finally had to accept could not remain in my life.

But if we are to help our children sustain loving and nurturing relationships in their adult years, it is vital that we teach them that loving someone should not hurt and that they can survive letting go of a person who is harmful to their spirits.

We also need to help our children understand that they cannot *save* anyone. While I believe we have a responsibility to try to alleviate the suffering of those who are in pain *when we can*, children who try to rescue troubled friends usually meet with disastrous results. Our kids are not meant to be saviors and should not be expected to take care of their friends, parents, or siblings, even though rescuing someone can feel oh so rewarding. If we instill in them the belief that it is their job to heal the people around them — whatever the personal cost — we send them down the painful road of people-pleasing from which it can take years to recover. There is a quote that eloquently captures this idea: *If you see a drowning man, reach out and try to pull him from the water. If he grabs your arm and tries to pull you in, push him as hard as you can.*

Help your children develop healthy boundaries — ones that reflect their self-respect and worth. If they have friends who are hurtful, explore with them whether the overall benefit of that relationship outweighs the costs. If they come to see that they deserve better, help them grieve the loss of that friendship — for it is a great loss to end a relationship that has had some value to us — so that they can effectively move on.

Listening to Intuition

In his book *Protecting the Gift*, security specialist Gavin de Becker shares numerous examples of crime victims ignoring their intuition despite sensing that they were in danger. De Becker believes it is essential that we listen to the intuitive messages that come in the form of hesitation, doubt, persistent thoughts, and nagging feelings. He explains that intuition's ultimate message is the one most difficult to ignore: fear. "But people try to silence even that one: *Calm down, calm down, it's probably nothing,* some tell themselves, rather than giving a fair hearing to nature's lifesaving signal." He goes on to say that "In fact, the root of the word intuition, *tueri*, means to guard and to protect."

If we are to raise confident children, we need to encourage them to listen to their inner wisdom and to trust their intuitive hunches. Our bodies are finely tuned instruments that can help us unravel the source of an upset, warn us when something isn't quite right, or alert us to potential danger. Sweaty palms, butterflies in the stomach, tension in the back of our neck, or a rapid heartbeat can all be indications that something is amiss. We may feel uncomfortable with someone's energy or sense that despite outward appearances, something isn't safe, even if everything looks "right." And of course the opposite is true: someone may appear disheveled or a situation may be different from what we expected but be perfectly fine. Intuition helps us discern whether all is well or whether we are at risk.

Share with your children the fact that our subconscious minds gather and sift through tremendous amounts of information to help us make decisions and that while we shouldn't ignore facts and figures, there is much to be gained from learning how to read intuitive signals and trusting our instincts.

If your daughter is upset about something going on with a friend, you might suggest, "Get quiet for a minute, honey, and see if you can tune in to your intuition. What do *you* feel is the best way to handle that problem with Elizabeth and Toni? Does it feel like a healthy relationship? Do you leave your time with them feeling good?" You can help this process along by offering a few of your thoughts, while inviting her to get still and tune in to how her body responds as you present each idea.

Our bodies tell us when we should be trusting, open, or guarded. Kids whose boundaries are respected have a much easier time setting them appropriately with their peers. Teach them that *no* is a complete sentence. Role-play scenarios in which they practice honoring their gut feeling when they are in an iffy situation, such as someone suggesting they try a beer when they don't feel ready or asking them to get sexually involved when they don't want to.

> *Kids whose boundaries are respected have a much easier time setting them appropriately with their peers. Teach them that* no *is a complete sentence.*

Impact Training is a fantastic program for teenage girls and women that helps them step out from the restraints of their socialization to be nice and helpful, encouraging them to declare their no in powerful ways. They also have programs for schoolchildren of both genders. I highly recommend it.

One of the ways I teach children to tune in to the subtler messages of their emotions is by asking them to describe their feelings in terms of colors. "If red is angry, black is sad, orange is happy, and so on, *What color are you feeling?*" In her book *Sitting Still Like a Frog,* Eline Snel asks children to tune in to their emotional state by inviting them to share their Personal Weather Report. *"What is the weather like right now in your body? Is it sunny or stormy?"* (For more on this technique, see chapter 11.)

Children should understand that it is normal to experience many different feelings, including anger. Keep a light plastic bat or punching bag on hand so your kids know that when they feel anger in their bodies, they can express it in safe and acceptable ways. It's *good* for our kids to stay present to the emotions in their bodies rather than shutting down, as so many of us did because our own parents told us not to be scared or hurt or mad.

We are each born with an inner toolbox of resources that we can draw on throughout our lives. Helping children learn to trust the internal compass of their intuition will help them steer away from trouble and toward beneficial opportunities.

Living with Passion

When I was sixteen, I worked after school at a day-care center. One day, four-year-old Ruby arrived. Her family had recently moved to Kansas City from India, and she knew not a word of English.

I thought it might be helpful if I learned a few Hindi words from her parents so I could ask little Ruby if she was hungry or needed to use the bathroom. From the moment my Hindi lesson began, something inside me started jumping up and down with joy. I *loved* this language. I practically inhaled our lessons, not wanting our time together to stop. As a sixteen-year-old living in Kansas in the 1970s, I didn't have a lot of options for learning this "exotic" language beyond imposing on the generosity of Ruby's parents who tutored me when they could find the time. I was so keen to learn that I began calling around the country, discovering that the University of Pennsylvania had a Hindi department. I ordered their textbook and waited eagerly until it arrived.

As soon as I received the book, I became a devoted student of Hindi. In the absence of having an actual teacher, I assigned myself exercises as homework, checking my answers at the back of the book. I devoured the material, and when I moved to New York at seventeen, I searched used bookstores for dictionaries and writing primers. When I ran out of those I could practice my Hindi with, I started calling people out of the phone book whose last name was Singh, asking them — in Hindi — if they would chat with me!

The best way I can describe this near obsession with learning Hindi was that I loved the way the words tasted in my mouth. An enormous happiness filled me whenever I studied, making it impossible to subdue the urge to learn.

This makes no sense — a teenage girl from Kansas passionately wanting to learn the language of people on the other side of the world. Yet learning Hindi opened doors for me that to this day continue to add something very special to my life. And of course when I have traveled in India, the experiences I've had because I speak the language (albeit imperfectly) have been extraordinary.

Consider how your children watch you using your time. If you carve out space for pursuing your passions — reading, painting, watching the stars, gardening — your children will see learning as an important part of life. And if you aren't sure what brings you joy, pursue the little things that catch your eye: a link on a Twitter feed, an interview on the radio, a headline on a magazine cover. Follow the bread crumbs, and they will carry you to where your heart wants you to go.

Fostering Curiosity

Each child comes with his or her unique built-in, preloaded passions. Some kids are consumed by a desire to dance their hearts out. Others want nothing more than to concoct culinary delights. Some want to tell stories, spend time with animals, or sketch inventions. If we want our children to discover their passion and purpose, we must stay open to what they drift toward rather than pushing them in directions *we* prefer they follow but that do not call to them.

> *If we want our children to discover their passion and purpose, we must stay open to what they drift toward rather than pushing them in directions we prefer they follow but that do not call to them.*

Doing this requires plenty of unstructured time and exposure to a variety of people and experiences. The endless organized activities we impose on our kids, coupled with pounds of nightly homework and the constant pull of their digital lives, often leaves no time for the quiet in which they might hear the voice leading them to *their* path of exploration. Had I not had free time in high school, I might never have pursued my desire to learn Hindi.

Packing a child's day from morning to night — and nowadays, weekends and summers — leaves them no time to wander, daydream, or explore the things that bring them alive.

Raising a child to be who he is meant to be also requires a commitment to fostering his fascination with life. I love the line from the contract that Janell Burley Hofmann wrote when she gave her thirteen-year-old son an iPhone: "Wonder without googling." In today's world, children rarely puzzle over things; the answer to any question is just seconds away, via whatever device is handy. But one of the greatest skills we can help our children develop is the capacity to solve problems. This requires settling into the not-knowing space generated between curiosity and answers.

Give your kids the opportunity to step outside traditional classroom walls and sniff out the things that interest them. These pursuits may not make sense at the time or even be long-lasting, but what a joy it is to follow the yearnings of the heart, as mysterious as they may be. When we do, all kinds of magic can happen.

> *By infusing your life with meaning and a passion for learning, and by providing your children with real-life opportunities to do the same, you will help inoculate them against ennui, apathy, and malaise, infusing their spirits with the joy that comes from pursuing the things that stir their souls.*

By infusing your life with meaning and a passion for learning, and by providing your children with real-life opportunities to do the same, you will help inoculate them against ennui, apathy, and malaise, infusing their spirits with the joy that comes from pursuing the things that stir their souls.

NOW IT'S YOUR TURN

Sit quietly and reflect on the following questions, recording your thoughts in your journal.

1. When you were a child what did you love to do? Did you enjoy playing outdoors? Painting? Making music? Writing poetry? Building things? Spending time with friends? Solving puzzles? Reading?
2. What do you love to do now? Or what would you do — simply for pleasure — if you had the time and freedom to pursue your passions?
3. In the past three months, how often have you engaged in an activity related to one of your passions? If your answer is "not at all," how long *has* it been since you spent time on something for pure pleasure?
4. What gets in the way of pursuing your hobbies, interests, or passions? We can all say, "No time," but go deeper with this question. Is that entirely true, or are there pockets of time when you *could* brush up on your piano or pick up a novel instead of flipping open your computer or watching TV?
5. How might your children benefit if you were to pursue one of your passions or interests?
6. Write down the amount of time you would like to dedicate to pursuing one of your passions and nourishing your spirit. Indicate which days might work best for adding this activity to your week, who might watch your kids, and any other details that might help ensure that this dream becomes a reality.

MAKING IT PRACTICAL
Parenting with Presence in Real Life

I have to be plugged in for work, so how do I model unplugging?

QUESTION: I understand the importance of limiting screen time, but I have a demanding boss who emails me at all hours of the day — and evening! He expects me to respond right away. I am very lucky that I get to work from home, and I don't want to lose my job. But my kids often see me turning on my computer or answering a text message when they thought we were having family time. How can I convince them that it's important to unplug when they see me switching on my device so often?

SUGGESTION: Technological advancements have made it possible for many parents to work from home, allowing them be there for their kids in day-to-day ways that were once impossible. But it also means that while it looks to your children as if all of you is present while you serve up breakfast or snuggle for a story, you may at any moment be interrupted by your employer, potentially leaving them feeling less important than whoever is behind those beeps. And as you mention, it may also seem hypocritical if you're encouraging your kids to unplug while you walk around with your smartphone glued to your ear.

Your situation is as much about giving your children the chance to vent about having to share you with your boss as it is about your use of technology. In my online courses and my previous book, *Parenting Without Power Struggles,* I teach something called Act I Parenting, a way of ensuring that our children feel heard before we come at them with explanations or advice.

I would say something like: "I wonder what it's like for you guys when you see Mommy answering her phone at dinner. Do you ever feel kinda mad about that?" Simply open up the conversation, making it clear that your kids get to have feelings about having to share you. Once they have gotten to vent, you may then say, "I get it. It doesn't seem fair when I answer the phone at dinner, especially when I'm so strict with you guys about shutting everything off so we can be together as a family. I can see where it wouldn't seem right." They will probably expect you to follow up with an explanation about your need for employment, but it may not be necessary if you've already given them the facts about your job and its requirements. What's most important is that they know it's safe to tell you their truth.

Your situation doesn't have a simple fix, short of finding a new job. In the meantime, if you acknowledge the frustrations your job sometimes creates rather than making a guilt-inducing remark if they complain — "You don't want Mommy to lose her job, do you?" — you will lessen the impact of being tied to your devices. Just be sure that when you *are* off work, you enjoy downtime with your kids in ways that don't involve a plug!

What if I have no time to create a supportive tribe?

QUESTION: I am a single mother of three children under the age of eight. My parents live on the other side of the country, and I have a full-time job. Since my divorce and our move to a new neighborhood, I haven't had time to meet the people next door, let alone form a supportive tribe of parents. I am very isolated.

SUGGESTION: Many parents are so busy that they hardly get to take a shower, let alone devote time to scouting out new friends. Still, I would encourage you to look for even the smallest opportunities to meet new people. You don't have to step too far outside the routines of daily life to bump up against others, but you may have to step outside your comfort zone to initiate conversation. Chat with another parent at morning drop-off, or establish a weekend ritual of taking your kids to a park where you'll have the chance to meet other parents in your neighborhood. Some find it helpful to ask their children's teachers to introduce them to the parents of classmates their child seems to like. Others take part in school happenings or attend local library events for kids.

Forging a tribe takes some effort, but the payoff is enormous, both for you and your children. We are not meant to go it alone or to parent in isolation. Take it slowly, perhaps setting an intention of meeting one new person a month. Over time, one person will introduce you to another, and before long you will have created your own network of support.

Can I prune out my ex-husband?

QUESTION: I agree that it is important to weed out the people in our lives who are hurtful to us, but what about my ex-husband? He is rude, unpredictable, and inconsiderate. I wish I could prune him from my life, but because of our custody arrangement, I have no choice but to deal with him almost every day.

SUGGESTION: As I've mentioned, we sometimes find ourselves with children whose behavior pushes our buttons, prompting us either to react out of old patterns or to rise to the challenge of working through unfinished business that ultimately helps us grow into a better version of ourselves. Certain adults also seem to have been custom designed to trigger us, often in circumstances like yours in which we cannot simply write them off.

Co-parenting after divorce is one of the hardest things a parent will ever have to do. On the one hand, you have parted ways with someone you once loved who has hurt or disappointed you so deeply that you can no longer tolerate living with them. You may feel rage, resentment, confusion, and profound sorrow. Naturally it would be less painful to wipe this person from your daily life. But this is where we get to practice all those declarations such as, "I'd take a bullet for my son" or "I'd move heaven and earth to keep my little girls safe."

You have a choice, every time you interact with your former husband. Will you focus on his unpleasant qualities, causing your stomach to tighten as you hiss out essential updates about your children? Or will you take out the magnifying glass to notice the good? I understand that focusing on his negative attributes may make it easier to come to terms with your divorce. But your children have endured a major loss, even if it was for the best. They need to be spared as much tension and strife between their mommy and daddy as possible.

Limit your contact as needed, but take the higher road. Don't take his behavior personally. Reach for compassion if you can, recognizing that on a deeper level — underneath his personality flaws or the hurts of your shared past — he is simply a fellow journeyer stumbling along on the path of life. By grieving for what you hoped you might have together or for the man you wish he was, you will be better able to accept your former husband as is, annoying faults and all.

My friend and colleague Katherine Woodward Thomas, creator of Conscious Uncoupling, reminds us that "we may be able to undo a marriage, but we can never undo a family without leaving the people in that family emotionally homeless." She admonishes us to put the needs of our child first by honoring how deeply he needs our permission and support to love and believe in his other parent, no matter how flawed that person might be. Learning to hold the complexity of your child's vulnerability with your own disappointment, and choosing to protect the emotional home your child has with your former spouse (in spite of your hurt), is the very essence of what it is to be a compassionate parent.

CHAPTER 6

Healthy Communication
Strengthens Connection

*Children have never been very good
at listening to their elders,
but they have never failed to imitate them.*

— JAMES A. BALDWIN

Some years ago I was on a safari in Tanzania. We had been driving for a day or two in search of a rhino, with no success. Our guide pulled the jeep into a rest area, where we would take a break and have lunch. Excited about the possibility of asking other Serengeti safari travelers if they had had any luck spotting this elusive animal, I said to the driver of the next jeep, "Have you seen any rhinos?" He mumbled something, clearly unhappy with my question, and went on his way. I asked our guide what the man had said and have never forgotten his answer. "He said that you did not greet him first."

I took the hit. He was absolutely right; I had rudely insinuated myself into this man's presence without so much as a *Hello, how are you?* I learned something priceless and am grateful that this man had the dignity and self-respect not to indulge my unconsciousness. I had forgotten my manners.

Modeling good manners is an essential ingredient in raising a child who becomes a confident, successful adult. I'm not talking about formal and complex rituals but simply the behaviors that make people feel comfortable. Some of us get hung up on the notion that teaching manners to kids is old-fashioned or only relevant to those living among royalty — rather unlikely for most of us. But I think the ability to put people at ease is as vital as having a diploma from a prestigious college. We may not know that our coworker graduated from Yale or Oxford, but we can immediately tell whether we feel relaxed and comfortable in her presence.

Modeling Good Manners

"Me first!" "I want more!" "Those are mine!" are all the normal expressions of a child who hasn't yet developed empathy or diplomacy. Children are naturally egocentric; if there's only one piece of pie left, they'll grab it. If your daughter is having fun on the swing set, she's going to resent giving it up to another child waiting for a turn. That doesn't mean she's selfish; it just means she's behaving like a child. A parent's uncritical guidance helps young ones learn the basics of showing concern about the wishes and needs of others.

There is no better way to teach good manners than to demonstrate them day in and day out in the presence of your children. For instance, at mealtimes ensure that no one begins eating until everyone has been seated and served. If your kids forget, let them know that you understand that they're hungry, while modeling patience as others dish up their food before you pick up your fork.

> There is no better way to teach good manners than to demonstrate them day in and day out in the presence of your children.

Help your children learn to share and take turns when they have a friend come over to play. Explain that you know it is hard to wait for a turn on the piano or to leave the bigger piece of cake for someone else, but that in your home, guests are treated with special care.

Teach your children how to introduce people. "Ms. Norris, I would like you to meet my cousin Joey" or "Grandpa, this is my friend Elsa." Make friendly greeting rituals part of the way you welcome guests into your home. Show your children how to make eye contact while offering a handshake to an arriving guest — or a hug, if appropriate and comfortable for your child.

Part of having good manners is acknowledging another person's feelings. When you show your children what it looks like to be accountable for an oversight or an inconsiderate remark, they will follow your lead. If you offend someone, let your kids hear you apologize, without justifying your behavior. Finally, make sure your youngsters know how to receive a compliment. "Thank you for that" is a simple, gracious way to take in someone's kind words and is much healthier than deflecting them.

> *When you show your children what it looks like to be accountable for an oversight or an inconsiderate remark, they will follow your lead.*

And don't save good manners for when company is around or those times when you're out in public. Children smell hypocrisy a mile away. Use those magic words — *please* and *thank you* — authentically when you speak with your loved ones. Peggy O'Mara, founder of *Mothering* magazine said, "Be careful how you speak to your children. One day, it will become their inner voice."

Children develop civility, thoughtfulness, and a considerate nature when they grow up in the midst of caring and respectful behavior. Acknowledge when your children exhibit good manners, and gently correct them when they forget. Don't expect them to behave perfectly, and make sure to factor in their developmental stage as you set expectations for their behavior.

And if you have a child with a developmental challenge or psychological issue, don't succumb to the guilt and shame that often show up when you imagine that others are judging you for your children's awkwardness or shortcomings. Get the loving support you need so that you know that your best is more than good enough, regardless of how your children behave.

Avoid creating power struggles about manners, especially with your teens. Trying to force a child to apologize or be polite will only backfire. With patience and loving guidance, your children will become the kind of people who make others comfortable. Ultimately, that's what good manners are all about.

Dealing with Anger

Parents often bring their children to me because of their problems with anger. Sometimes the child has a difficult time managing his outbursts because his capacity to manage big feelings is underdeveloped because of immaturity or impulsive tendencies. But often I discover that Mom or Dad also have big tempers.

All of us — children and adults alike — are subject to strong emotions that we cannot always control. Some people are easygoing, hardly ruffled when life doesn't go their way. But others struggle to keep frustration and disappointment from wreaking emotional havoc. If the root cause of anger is not addressed, we sometimes end up doing or saying things we regret. Using threats or punishments to deter our children from acting out angrily can drive unresolved emotions underground, where they can show up as eating disorders, addiction, or depression. It can also stockpile the fuel for a bigger explosion of rage later on.

Instead of shaming ourselves when we lose our cool, we need to step back, determine what we're thinking or feeling, and identify the underlying source of our rage. Anger can be the outward manifestation of unresolved grief, sadness, frustration, stress, hormonal imbalance, anxiety, or fatigue. Until we understand that it is a symptom of something that needs to be addressed rather than a voluntary behavior, we will not be able to diminish its impact on our lives.

When I am working with a family in which angry outbursts are commonplace, I find it helpful to facilitate conversations between the yeller and the yellee (the target of the rage) in a way that makes it safe for both to be heard.

> *Until we understand that anger is a symptom of something that needs to be addressed rather than a voluntary behavior, we will not be able to diminish its impact on our lives.*

When both parties can lay down their defenses and step into the other's shoes for a few moments, they become more willing to work on resolving whatever emotions are fueling their flare-ups.

I also tell the following story (author unknown):

A young boy had a very bad temper; he often lashed out in anger at those around him. One day his father gave him a bag of nails and told him that each time he lost his temper, he was to go hammer a nail into the fence.

The first few days, the boy had to hammer lots of nails into the fence. But as time went on, he gradually found that he could catch himself before he lost his temper. Knowing that he would have to find a nail and take it to the backyard to hammer it into the fence helped him manage his angry outbursts.

Finally, the boy came to a point where he was able to tell his father that he had learned how to stop himself from losing his temper. His father said that each time he was able to get through a day without hurting others with his anger, he could remove a nail from the fence.

The day arrived when the boy went to his father to tell him that all the nails were now gone.

The father led his son to the fence and said, "You have learned something very important, son. But I want

you to look at the holes in the wood. This fence will never
be the same as it was before the nails were hammered into
it. In the same way, when you say things in anger — even
if you apologize — your words and actions leave a scar
like these holes in the fence. "

We need to help our children learn to lengthen the gap
between having an impulse to say or do something and acting on
that impulse. To err *is* human and to forgive, divine. But as children deepen their understanding that, like nails in the fence, our
actions have irreversible consequences and can harm important
relationships, we can help them take steps toward slowing down
when they are upset, taking responsibility for their actions, and
making amends when needed.

The damage done by cruel words and hurtful behaviors cannot be undone. Whenever we argue with others, we need to pause
and consider the effects our words might have on them.

Telling the Truth

There are some great scenes in the show *The Newsroom* in which
Jim, a genteel young man, has been dating Lisa, with whom he
was fixed up by Maggie, despite his protestations. Because Jim is
so well-mannered, he continues dating Lisa despite feeling that he
has little in common with her. He is in fact much more interested
in Maggie. (It's complicated.) Jim and Lisa's relationship continues for months. Maggie even buys gifts and a romantic card for
Jim to give to Lisa for Valentine's Day, solidifying Lisa's attachment to Jim. Lisa finally tells Jim that she loves him, and because
he is so polite, he says he loves her, too. The relationship becomes
even more serious, while Jim suffers in silence. He knows that he
should tell Lisa the truth but can't bear to hurt her feelings.

Finally, Lisa happens to overhear the truth about how Jim

feels about her, and about his affection for Maggie, and she confronts him. Even as he is being given the opportunity to fess up, Jim denies what she has heard. Wisely, Lisa says, "Jim, admit it. We could be choosing preschools for our children before you worked up the courage to tell me how you really feel!" She convinces him that she would rather know the truth than be in make-believe love, and he finally lets go.

It is not easy to navigate difficult conversations, especially about sensitive issues, but if we want our child to have healthy grown-up relationships, then teaching her the art of speaking her truth is crucial. It is helpful if our children routinely hear us clearing up problems with our loved ones with opening lines like, "Something has been bothering me…" "I'm not sure what you meant when you said…" "I've been having a hard time with…" "I don't really like it when…"

Most of us have read enough self-help books to know that one of the keys to maintaining a great relationship is good communication. But what does that look like? As mentioned, my *Act I Parenting* strategy helps parents come *alongside* rather than *at* their children so they will be receptive to their guidance instead of clenching and resisting. This approach involves validating the child's experience rather than trying to talk her out of her feelings. The same holds true for anyone we are communicating with; when we are forceful in conveying our point of view, we engender resistance in the other person.

Good communication requires that we acknowledge the other person's position, recognizing that he has as much right to his feelings as we have to ours, instead of trivializing his opinion or arguing him out of his feelings when they differ from our own. It means taking responsibility for how we communicate, expressing our concerns in a way that doesn't cast blame or make the other person wrong.

> *Good communication creates space for hurts or grievances to be aired and truths to be told. It fosters intimacy, even if getting there is uncomfortable as difficult feelings are brought out into the open.*

Good communication creates space for hurts or grievances to be aired and truths to be told. It fosters intimacy, even if getting there is uncomfortable, as difficult feelings are brought out into the open. It provides an avenue for needs to be met or at least negotiated. It helps us get to know others — and ourselves. And it allows us to receive important feedback from those who are important to us — if we can step out of our ego to receive it. These are all qualities we want our children to possess as they grow.

Listening Respectfully

We can coach our children to express their wishes without aggression and to listen respectfully to others. But as I have said again and again, we have to show them what that looks like for it to stick. Telling your child not to interrupt or roll her eyes will mean nothing if you and your partner interrupt and roll your eyes at each other when you don't see eye to eye.

I once read that before you speak, you should ask yourself three things:

1. Is it true?
2. Is it necessary?
3. Is it kind?

By infusing your communications with care and consciousness, you cannot help but raise children who are more aware of the impact of their words and for whom an internal bell rings when they or someone else speaks in a hurtful way.

In my clinical practice, I often facilitate listening practices between a parent and child, choosing a topic that regularly generates conflict. The rules of the game are simple: One person speaks for two to three minutes, sharing their thoughts and feelings about the topic in question. The listener faces the speaker with open body language and is not allowed to interrupt, grimace, disagree, or in any way disparage what the speaker is expressing.

When the speaker is finished talking, the listener has to ask questions or make comments that generate three yeses. This exercise almost never fails to bring parent and child closer, because each has been given the chance to *safely* express themselves and feel heard. It is very easy to do and not only helps family members feel more connected but also paves the way for children to develop the skill of negotiating conversations that allow both parties to feel understood. In chapter 11 you'll find an example of this type of dialogue.

> *Telling your child not to interrupt or roll her eyes will mean nothing if you and your partner interrupt and roll your eyes at each other when you don't see eye to eye.*

Connecting through Chitchat

I want to touch on another topic related to communication, one that may surprise you: small talk. For much of my life, I thought that chitchat was a rather frivolous and unenlightened activity. Sharing opinions about the weather or the tastiest brand of yogurt felt silly. But as I have gotten older, I have come to see things differently.

We are a social species. When human beings come together, we have an instinct to connect. But how? We can certainly meet someone and gaze wordlessly into their eyes. But brief conversations are lovely ways to exchange energy. The topic itself is irrelevant. A discussion about the weather simply serves as a vehicle for making contact, conveying, "I see you. I am here with you. I'm interested in you."

It is helpful to teach our children how to dialogue with others so they can participate in short exchanges with whomever they might meet. I can't count the times I have seen kids freeze up when someone tries to engage them in conversation. "What do you like to do, Bobby?" "I don't know." "Do you enjoy sports?" "I guess."

So while I am not a proponent of routinely superficial conversation, I do believe there is a time and a place for a friendly chat and that we do our children no favors when we shield them by saying, "Sorry, she doesn't want to talk." Yes, some of us are introverts who are uncomfortable with social contact, legitimately shy creatures who find it painful to even look at someone we don't know, let alone strike up a conversation. I'm not suggesting that we force our kids to be who they aren't, and I'm certainly not proposing that we encourage them to chat up random strangers. But if we are to equip our youngsters with the skills they will need to grow into conscious, confident adults, then we need to teach them the art of conversation, according to their particular capabilities.

NOW IT'S YOUR TURN

Think about a situation in which communication broke down with someone important to you, resulting in angry words, resentment, or perhaps even estrangement.

How did you contribute to the conversation taking a turn for the worse? Did you come *at* the other person with your guns blazing? Whenever you start a sentence with, "Why did you…" you're almost guaranteed to elicit defensiveness in the other person. Did you passively agree to whatever the other person said, secretly fuming but refusing to express how you really felt?

Take a few minutes to reflect on how you might have approached this difficult conversation differently. How could you have made it clear that you were open to the other person's point of view? How might you have expressed your feelings honestly but respectfully, leading to a better outcome? You may want to record your thoughts in your journal.

MAKING IT PRACTICAL
Parenting with Presence in Real Life

How can I correct my son without shaming him?

QUESTION: How do you help a child understand that his words and actions can hurt others without leaving him feeling ashamed? My son has problems with impulsivity as well as a bad temper, but he is also a very sensitive child. He feels terrible after he has had a tantrum, announcing that he hates himself. How can we help him work on not having major meltdowns without shaming him?

SUGGESTION: This scenario is often played out with children who are both sensitive and impulsive. On the one hand, they may have a thin skin and be especially vulnerable to hurts and slights. On the other, they may have poor brakes on the car in terms of their impulse control, skidding into meltdowns before they can stop themselves.

There is no simple solution to your dilemma. It is good for your son to feel some regret for his outbursts because remorse acts as an inhibiting influence on behavior. If he feels bad about lashing out at his sibling, for instance, he may be better able to restrain himself the next time he gets upset. The problem is that while this idea works in theory, children with impulsivity issues usually don't have the emotional maturity to thoughtfully weigh out the pros and cons of lashing out before they find themselves doing it. Their fuse is short; they feel angry, and in a flash, they have exploded.

When children feel shame for not being able to control themselves in the midst of an emotional storm, they need to know that *they are not their behavior*. Help your son see the person he is — someone who doesn't like hurting others — as separate from his disturbing behavior. This doesn't mean he isn't responsible for his actions, but it does allow him to know that he is a fine and valuable human being, apart from the way he acts. Help him to recognize the warning signs of an emotional hurricane in his body — tightness in his belly or rapid heartbeats — so that he can ask you for help before his storms do damage.

Should introverted children be made to chitchat?

QUESTION: You talk about encouraging children to strike up conversations with others, but my daughter is extremely shy. She can hardly look people in the eye when they come to our house, although once she gets to know them she is terrific. Shouldn't we let introverted kids be who they are rather than forcing them to chat with people when it pains them so?

SUGGESTION: Yes, we should let introverted kids be who they are; we should let all kids be who they are. But no child *wants* to be crippled with anxiety when faced with interacting with others.

This question is difficult to answer because some kids need a gentle nudge, while others genuinely cannot and should not be drawn out. Far be it from me to suggest that a child significantly on the autism spectrum, for instance, should be scolded for not chatting with the cashier at the market.

Trust yourself. If your child is incapable of engaging in social intercourse, than by all means, let her be. But if she is simply inexperienced in opening up a conversation or establishing rapport, perhaps you will consider helping her become more comfortable in this area.

Should I ask my husband to apologize?

QUESTION: My husband and I don't agree when it comes to apologizing to our children after we have yelled at them. I usually feel terrible afterward and I tell my kids that I'm sorry. But my husband is very proud. Even when he tells me that he does feel bad after he has yelled, he thinks it is a sign of weakness to apologize to them.

SUGGESTION: Being married to someone does not guarantee that we will see eye to eye on every aspect of child rearing. Even if we determined that we were mostly in sync with our partner before having children together, there are still countless opportunities to disagree.

Chances are your husband is patterning his behavior on that of his father or of an important role model from his childhood. These early impressions are powerful. Don't lecture, advise, berate, or criticize him for his unwillingness to apologize to your children. If you come across as his scolding, shaming parent, you will only flip on the switch of his resistance.

If your husband sees you acting with integrity around your kids — meaning he observes you taking responsibility for your actions — and subsequently notices your children being respectful and cooperative with you, he may eventually conclude that apologizing is a sign of strength, not weakness. But you will have to let him find his own way. If you judge him, he will only more staunchly defend his actions.

CHAPTER 7

• Walking the Talk •

*The greatest way to live with honor in this world
is to be what we pretend to be.*

— SOCRATES

I once read about a tribe in Africa whose members do something quite extraordinary when somebody does something wrong. They believe that every person comes into the world wanting love and peace but that sometimes people make mistakes. For two days the whole tribe surrounds the wrongdoer, telling him everything good he has done in his life. They view the man's transgression as a cry for help and come together to hold him up and remind him of who he is, until he remembers the core goodness from which he temporarily became disconnected.

Consider what might happen if we did *that* with kids who are troubled or hurting? Imagine compassionately reminding them of their goodness instead of berating them when they make a mistake? When we know that we are loved even after we have lost our way, it is far easier for us to acknowledge our wrongdoing and look for ways to make amends, restoring the trust of those we care about.

> *When we know that we are loved even after we have lost our way, it is far easier for us to acknowledge our wrongdoing and look for ways to make amends, restoring the trust of those we care about.*

Modeling Consistent Behavior

How you do anything is how you do everything. This has been a fundamentally important concept in my life, one that has influenced me both personally and professionally.

When my son was ten, he asked me why I had been rude to a telemarketer who had called during dinner. "Would you have acted that way if he was sitting in front of you?" he asked. "No, honey... of course not."

When people say that your kids will hold you to high standards, they aren't kidding. They see us at our best and our worst; everything we do makes an impression. The way we speak to a telemarketer or follow through on a promise to help with a science project is all duly noted by our children. We may forget our manners, or find we don't have time after all to help as promised with a science project. That's okay; we're human, and will inevitably fall short of who we most want to be now and again.

But when we behave in a way that doesn't line up with what we preach to our children, we need to take responsibility. "I meant to allow time to help you with that project, and I can see that I'm letting you down." Or, in the case of my son and the telemarketer, "I could give you excuses about why I spoke to that fellow rudely, but you're right. I don't feel good about how I was with him."

Adhering to the notion that how we do anything is how we do everything can be a real burden. We have to be willing to forgive ourselves — often. But by demonstrating consistency in our character, we establish ourselves as a reliable North Star, worthy of being a reference point for our children as they navigate their lives with honor and integrity.

Being Accountable

Teaching our children to be accountable for how they show up in the world — on their good days and their not-so-good ones

— gives them an enormous advantage in life. We are all drawn to people we can trust — those who follow through on their commitments and keep their word — and we trust those who take responsibility for their actions.

Fifteen-year-old Sean came to see me after a blowout argument with his mother, during which he had called her some pretty ugly names. I asked him to tell me the story of what had led to him getting grounded for a month. His story went like this: "She made me really mad so I said #$%*. Then she said I was grounded for a week! I got madder and told her I thought she was @^&*!. And *then* she said I was grounded for *another* week and so I said *#$%."

When I asked Sean how he'd felt about it afterward, he told me that he felt pretty bad, but he was also upset that he'd been grounded.

I asked if I could offer him my take on what he had just shared with me. "I get the impression that you felt kind of forced to say hurtful things because your mom was upsetting you. Is that how you see it?"

He agreed. But he smiled a little; he knew me well enough to know that I was probably going to encourage him to step outside his version of events to see things from a wider perspective.

I said, "Sean, can you tell me the same story, but this time, as you describe what you did or said, please first use the words *I decided to* or *I chose to*."

He squirmed a little, but he was a good sport. "My mom made me really mad when she was coming down on me about something so *I decided to* say #$%* to her. She got really mad and said I was grounded for a week. So I got even madder and *chose* to tell her I thought she was @^&*!. Then she got super mad at me and said I was grounded for two weeks, so I *decided to* say *#$%."

When he finished, I asked him how it felt to tell the second version of his story. Poor guy — it was so much easier to blame his mom than to claim ownership for his contribution to the situation. To his credit, though, he admitted that he had made some pretty bad choices, which had led to him getting in trouble. I talked about how we all make mistakes, but that if own up to them and commit to making amends, we can set things right again.

> *Nothing helps children understand the implications of poor life choices like hearing stories from people who are putting their lives back together after having radically lost their way.*

It is all well and good to talk to our children about the importance of facing the consequences of bad decisions in the hopes that they will be thoughtful and prudent with the choices they make. But nothing helps them understand the implications of poor life choices like hearing stories from people who are putting their lives back together after having radically lost their way.

A client of mine takes his kids to buy their Christmas tree at a lot run by residents of a residential recovery program called Delancey Street. This father told me, "We are all inspired by our experiences with Delancey Street residents. A man helping us choose our tree might talk about his kids who he hasn't seen in two years. He tells us, 'It's worth it, because if I stay with this program, I will finally be able to be the father they deserve.' Another time we may discover that the guy joking with us as we tie the tree to the roof of the car has spent the majority of his life in prison. He talks about the mistakes he made, and how grateful he is to still be alive and to have the chance to start over." My client has taken his children to buy their Christmas tree from Delancey Street for years, in part because he sees what a positive effect it has on them to talk with people who have taken responsibility for the mistakes they have made and who are turning their lives around.

Understandably, most of us try to insulate our children from people who are struggling with addiction or the aftermath of dishonest dealings. But if you have trusted friends who are on the other side of a difficult life patch and are doing well, it can be invaluable to let your kids listen to their hard-earned advice. Whether sitting around a fire thousands of years ago, or standing in a suburban Christmas tree lot, we humans learn best from the stories of others. Exposing children to the wisdom and insight of people who lost and then found their way after facing their mistakes can make a big impact on their lives.

Motivating Children to Tell the Truth

All children fiddle with the truth; at certain ages it is developmentally appropriate. In fact, distorting the truth is part of learning the difference between fantasy and reality, fact and fiction. And of course kids hide the truth to avoid getting in trouble. The discomfort of perpetuating a deception is usually more tolerable than suffering the consequences of admitting a difficult truth, even at the risk of getting caught later. Later is later, and now is now.

Rather than using fear and shame to encourage children to own up to their mistakes, we serve our kids better when we emphasize (and of course model) how much better it feels to be honest, even when it is difficult to do so.

A study done at the University of Toronto in 2010 explored the factors that motivate children to be truthful. Children aged three to seven were left alone in a room after being told not to peek at a mystery toy. The researchers soon after returned to the room and read aloud a story — *Pinocchio, The Boy Who Cried Wolf*, or *George Washington and the Cherry Tree*. They then asked the children if they had peeked at the hidden toy.

The children who had just listened to a story with negative consequences for dishonesty were told, "I don't want you to be like Pinocchio or the boy who cried wolf; tell me the truth!" The children who heard the story about George Washington admitting that he had indeed chopped down the cherry tree were asked to be like him. These children were three times as likely to confess to having peeked as the ones who heard about a negative result of lying — the shame of Pinocchio's nose growing or the boy who cried wolf being eaten.

In an interesting twist, when the ending of the George Washington story was changed so that instead of confessing to his father that he had chopped down the cherry tree he lied and said he had not, the children who heard the revised version were as unwilling to confess to peeking at the mystery toy as those who had heard stories in which dishonesty led to a negative consequence.

> *Children are more likely to admit to a mistake when they think of honesty as a positive quality than if they think of dishonesty as something that leads to a bad result.*

The results suggest that children are more likely to admit to a mistake when they think of honesty as a positive quality than if they think of dishonesty as something that leads to a bad result. In other words, fear of punishment is a weaker motivator than the promise of praise and approval.

Apologizing

In my parenting life, I realized that although I didn't have to be perfect, I did have to learn how to take responsibility for those times when I lost my cool and said or did things that were beneath me. I had to learn how to *apologize*.

This was a difficult process because my ego had generated many strategies to avoid being wrong. I had grown up in an environment that valued Being Right over acknowledging one's shortcomings and was trained in the art of defending yourself, a graduate from the school of Justifications, Rationalizations, and Blaming Others.

Remember when I said that our children can be our greatest teachers? It was my son who provided me with the opportunity to discover that I could relax into the blessed experience of being imperfect. I could own up to my mistakes. It was a slow process, but *what a relief!* And there was an enormous side benefit: I was now raising a young man who willingly apologized when he messed up, demonstrating that he valued love over winning an argument or being right.

This is what I have learned about apologies. They must be genuine; I have no interest in forcing children to reluctantly mumble, "I'm sorry" after they have hurt somebody's feelings or body. In fact, an insincere apology teaches children that it's okay to *be a jerk* (that's a clinical term!), as long as they mutter those two little words. It is essential that our children deliver an apology only after they have come to feel genuine remorse.

This cannot happen in the context of shame. When we humiliate our child for slipping up, her defense mechanisms kick in, making it harder for her to admit to any wrongdoing. Instead we must gently help our children be exposed to the injured heart of another so they can consider the impact of their unkind behavior. Only then can they deliver an authentic "I'm sorry," or make some gesture of reparation.

> *We must gently help our children be exposed to the injured heart of another so they can consider the impact of their unkind behavior.*

The first step in apologizing is to say, "I'm sorry" from your heart, without tagging on a justification for your behavior. "I'm sorry, but I only stepped on your foot because it was sticking out too far" is not an apology. Many people are good at delivering a superficial apology, but they neutralize the impact by explaining why they did what they did, often including the other person as a causal factor. "I'm sorry I got mad when you were late, but I was worried sick! And I'm so tired...

and the vegetables are overcooked...and the dog trampled the roses..." is not the same as, "I'm so sorry I got so angry when you walked in late." Period. See the difference? There may be a time when you talk about what happened in a way that helps the other person see the ways he may have contributed to the problem. But the initial exchange is about taking the sting out of *your* behavior.

Second, we need to *specifically* acknowledge how our behavior affected the other person. "It must have really hurt your foot when I stepped on it." Or, "When I shouted at you the minute you walked in the door, you probably felt blindsided, especially when you had been sitting in traffic for an hour." This lets the injured party know that we aren't just intellectually spouting out words that sound good but that we have actually put ourselves in her shoes and can imagine the specific ways she might have been affected by our actions.

Third, we reveal how we felt as a result of our mistake, sharing our intention to do better. "I felt wretched afterward — embarrassed that I lost my cool. I want you to know that I'm really working on this. I love you and don't want you to worry that if you're running late, I might launch into a yelling episode." Here you may choose to share what you are doing to minimize the likelihood that this behavior will repeat itself — whether it's committing to leave the room when you become upset, counting to ten, journaling, working with a therapist, or getting more sleep.

Finally, you ask the other party what he needs in order to forgive you and to feel better. "Is there anything you need from me?" This lets the other person tell you that she appreciates your apology and is ready to move on or gives her permission to express what she would like from you. For example, she might say, "I want to forgive you, but I'd like you to assure me that the next time I'm running late and my phone isn't getting service, you will listen to what happened before unleashing your anger."

Someone once told me that at their child's preschool, little ones are specifically taught not to say, "I'm sorry" when they hurt another child. Instead, they are instructed to ask their friend if she is okay and to show their concern by bringing her a cup of water and a damp paper towel (for their boo-boo.) Anyone who witnessed the accident is also encouraged to bring a damp paper towel to the injured child. So whenever a child in that school is injured, he or she is provided with a cup of water and a pile of damp paper towels! I love the image of a little boy or girl wiping their tears while surrounded by a group of small children helping them feel better. These children are learning at a very young age how to take practical steps toward making amends when a mistake has been made rather than just mumbling a disingenuous, "Sorry..."

To sum up, here are the four steps of delivering an apology:

1. "I'm sorry," spoken from the heart and without any explanations, which might be seen as an attempt to justify or defend what happened.

2. "I imagine you felt _____," showing that you have stepped into the other person's shoes with empathy and concern.

3. "In the future..." Here is where you announce your intention to do better, making it clear that your hurtful behavior is not something you want to repeat.

4. "Is there anything you need from me?" You are inviting the other person to share whatever might be preventing him from forgiving you and moving on.

As we begin to acknowledge our mistakes instead of defending ourselves or blaming others when we lose our way, we gain a tremendous sense of freedom. Without having to struggle over the mismatch between the more evolved person we would like to be and the invariably flawed one we occasionally show up as, we can accept ourselves with greater compassion. Each apology comes easier, and ironically, putting aside defensiveness allows us to empathize more sincerely.

Parenting helps us face our foibles and take responsibility for our actions rather than letting pride and ego run the show, helping us raise children who are accountable for their behavior and who understand the importance of living with integrity.

NOW IT'S YOUR TURN

Before we begin I'd like to make it clear that the purpose of the following exercise is not to reactivate old shame or regret but rather to explore the fact that it is often more painful and costly to repress or hide a mistake than it is to admit it and make amends.

Think about a mistake you made that prompted an important life lesson.

In your journal, describe the situation.

Was anyone hurt? If so, how?

Did you immediately address the fallout from this mistake, or did you initially deny having made it and hope that no one found out?

If you did not address your mistake, what did it cost you to withhold the truth?

What amends did you make to whomever was affected by this mistake?

If it's appropriate and would not harm anyone, share this story with your child, helping her understand the lesson you learned from facing your mistake.

Summarize any thoughts or reflections from this exercise in your journal.

MAKING IT PRACTICAL
Parenting with Presence in Real Life

Shouldn't children be punished for misbehaving?

QUESTION: That story about the tribe in Africa is heartwarming, but I don't understand how we can help children learn to behave properly if we don't punish them when they have been bad. Isn't it confusing to them? Shouldn't a child face negative consequences for misbehaving, instead of being told that he is a good person?

SUGGESTION: When we equate a child with his disobedient behavior, we do him a great disservice. Human beings do things for one of two reasons: either to experience pleasure or to avoid pain. A person who lies, steals, or harms others does so either because he believes that his actions will somehow make him feel better — more powerful, respected, or vindicated — or because he thinks they will help him avoid some form of pain.

Children who are consistently judged, scolded, shamed, or beaten down for their mistakes are not inspired to do better. They often give up, justifying their misdeeds because their hearts have become hardened. (Psychologists have a term for this: *dry-eyed syndrome.*) By reminding a child of the goodness of his spirit and maintaining a clear vision of who he is at his core, we help restore his faith in himself. This is far more effective in helping children develop the courage to do the right thing than threatening punishment.

This is not to say there should never be natural consequences for a child's mistakes or misdeeds. If Eliza has gone on a rampage through the house, creating upheaval because she wasn't allowed to wear her sister's sweater, you may decide not to take her to the park. But as you have probably figured out by now, my approach to misbehavior is to look at its underlying causes rather than to think in terms of punishments (or rewards.) I don't believe Band-Aid solutions are effective; I'm far more interested in understanding why a child's misbehavior makes its own kind of sense — and addressing it at its root — than arbitrarily delivering punishments when a child has behaved poorly.

Is it normal for children to lie?

QUESTION: My ten-year-old has turned into a habitual liar who makes up stories to avoid getting in trouble. I never know when he's telling the truth and when he's fibbing, so I have to assume he is lying and punish him appropriately. Of course this makes him furious when he has actually been honest. How can I tell the difference?

SUGGESTION: When a child misbehaves, I put on my detective hat and ask one of these questions: Why does his behavior make sense? What would have to be true for him to decide to lie? What pleasure is the child looking for, or what pain is he trying to avoid? What is the payoff for lying? Chances are he is avoiding the pain of getting in trouble. That makes sense, right?

I often say that we *teach* our children how honest they can be with us based on how we react when they tell us things we don't want to hear. What happens when your son *does* tell you the truth? Do you get furious? Do you express grave disappointment in him? Does he feel ashamed and embarrassed? Humiliated? This is not to say that it's your "fault" that your son is dishonest, or that he shouldn't be accountable for his deceptiveness. But when I'm working with a dishonest child, I always start by assuming that he is making what feels to him to be the best of two bad choices.

It hurts children to lie to their loved ones, violating a sense of closeness and connection that is fundamentally important to them. But if your son feels that disappointing you with the truth will feel even worse (or he fears your wrath and punishments), he will probably continue to think lying is the lesser of two evils.

The more you can work toward becoming that Captain of the ship who comes across as capable of hearing difficult truths from your son, the less he will try to protect you (and himself) by lying.

You may also find it useful to read about strengthening attachment and connection between the two of you. When children feel liked, seen, and enjoyed by us, their natural instinct to cooperate and connect is awakened, and they find it much harder to tolerate the discomfort of being dishonest.

QUESTION: My father tried his best with us kids (my mom wasn't around), but I was an angry and wild teenager; I hung around with some tough kids and did some things I'm not proud of, like blowing up mailboxes and spraying graffiti around town. I turned my life around, and I want my kids — nine and eleven — to look up to their dad. Should I tell them about what I did?

SUGGESTION: Most of us have done things that reflect a temporary loss of our moral compass. While it's hard to completely shake off that horrible knot in the stomach when we remember the times we acted badly, what matters most is where you are today. It sounds as if you are invested in creating a life that reflects the man you want to be, and that is what's most important.

Far be it from me to decide what you tell your children, and when. There is no right answer to your question, at least from my vantage point. My best advice is to listen to your instincts about whether to share with your children what your earlier choices cost you. It may be beneficial to let them know the pain you feel when you call to mind some of the things you did as a teen. Just be sure it is in their best interests to share details, rather than a way to expunge your guilt. Do not make your children your confessors.

And if you decide not to tell your kids about your transgressions, be clear about doing so for the right reasons — because you don't think they are ready to integrate that old version of their father with the one they know today.

If you need to right a wrong — send a letter of apology, make restitution, pay off a debt — do so; it is never too late to make amends. I hope that you not only take responsibility for your choices but that you also forgive yourself. As Maya Angelou said, "When we know better, we do better." It sounds like you know better now, and will raise children who make better choices.

CHAPTER 8

Cultivating Empathy, Vulnerability, and Compassion

*Our human compassion binds us the one to the other —
not in pity or patronizingly, but as human beings
who have learnt how to turn our common
suffering into hope for the future.*

— Nelson Mandela

At first glance, we are a diverse species. There are roughly 6,500 spoken languages in the world today. That is a lot of variation in the way we put words to our hopes, needs, fears, and dreams.

But those hopes, needs, fears, and dreams? They are essentially the same. We are one species stumbling around on this whirling planet, trying to survive, to keep our kids alive, and to make our time here as meaningful as possible.

Sometimes I picture all of humanity as seeds of life, scattered over the globe. We may eat different foods or have varied shades to our skin, but we are members of the same tribe. If we are to survive as a species, our children need to grow up knowing that we are

> *If we are to survive as a species, our children need to grow up knowing that we are interconnected at the most cellular and primal level.*

interconnected at the most cellular and primal level. The world is in a fragile place; the capacity to show care and compassion toward our fellow human beings is critical to our preservation.

More than twenty years ago, while observing monkeys' brains, Italian researchers Giacomo Rizzolatti and Vittorio Gallese discovered what they called "mirror neurons." They noticed that certain brain cells were activated when a monkey reached out and grabbed a peanut and that a subset of motor cells was also activated when that monkey watched *another* monkey reach out to grab a peanut. In other words, even though the monkey was not personally carrying out an action, his brain responded as though it were.

Scientific research now supports the notion that mirror neurons are triggered in our brains when someone else is sad, angry, or happy, helping us feel what the other person is feeling as though we were in her place. Mirror neurons are now thought to be vital to human empathy, allowing us to regard our fellow human beings with tenderness — feeling what they feel. In other words, we are hardwired to experience empathy. That said, I believe there are things we can do either to advance our children's capacity to tune in to the feelings of others or to further the tendency in some to insulate themselves.

Listening to Others' Stories

Not long ago my son launched a project and website called *Letters to Our Former Selves*, inviting people to write letters to younger versions of themselves with insights, advice, or comfort based on the perspective they had gained from being further along in their lives. The idea was to re-create the sort of conversations around the fire that humankind has shared for millennia. His initial intention was to create a place for the cross-pollination of wisdom, where he and his peers might learn from their elders — and perhaps those elders could learn a thing or two from the youngsters. As he has collected letters from people of all different ages and cultures, I have witnessed in him a quiet transformation. He is becoming more openhearted.

I always told my son stories about people less advantaged than we were, and whenever possible, exposed him to well-traveled people who could enlighten him about the world beyond our backyard. He was barely three when we first took him to India; we went again when he was seven and again when he was ten. When he was fifteen, I took him on a two-and-a-half-month trip to Uganda, Tanzania, Australia, and New Zealand to explore, learn, and volunteer. In college he spent a semester living with a family in Senegal. I know that these experiences helped him become a compassionate young man, comfortable with people from all walks of life.

But reading letters written with such raw vulnerability has significantly awakened his own. He finishes conversations more often with, "I love you." Sometimes he calls just to thank me for talking him through something or putting together a great dinner. I see him making more effort to appreciate and nurture his other important relationships as well.

One letter in particular really broke something open for Ari. It was from a young man — a Chinese immigrant — written to himself as a young boy.

Dear Z,

Stop staring at that lunchbox. Its contents are nothing to be ashamed of.

Bok choy, rice, and stir fry; your mother woke up early to make it for you. She bought the ingredients at the grocery store, boiled them, fried them, and packed them neatly into a box. She didn't do it to spite you, and she didn't do it because she's a stubborn Chinese woman who refuses to assimilate. She did it because she wanted you to have a home-cooked meal, because she recognizes that look of loneliness on your face when she drops you off at school every morning.

Stop hiding your chopsticks; you're not convincing anybody by using a fork. The kid sitting next to you won't stop throwing his pencil at you if you try to act more American. They're not going to stop calling you names every day when you walk through the door, and they're not going to stop hating you if you pretend to be more like them.

Someday you'll understand that they don't hate you at all. They hate themselves, they hate their lives, and they hate the cruel hand of fate that birthed them into destitution. They're just not mature enough to know better, so they take their hate, their venomous self-loathing, and pour it onto you. They pour it on you because they see your vulnerability, your uncertainty, and your confusion from moving into this strange land.

Be strong, Z. Pick up your chopsticks, and eat your lunch. Eat it proudly, eat it with your back straight and your head held high. Because you'll live to eat lunches made by grand chefs, lunches fit for kings, and lunches in exotic lands. But they'll never taste anything as sweet as the lunch you ate the day you learned to take pride in yourself.

Letters like these allow us a glimpse of another person's private trials and triumphs. They remind us that there are always options, that we can change our minds, make different choices, and create for ourselves a life in alignment with our heart and soul.

Developing Compassion

Compassion and vulnerability go hand in hand. We cannot legislate kindness in our children, nor should we punish them when they fail to show empathy to others. For their hearts to soften, they have to spend time outside the bubble we sometimes so carefully construct and guard. And they also need to watch us living compassionate lives.

When we seek opportunities to make the world smaller for our kids, it helps them recognize themselves as global citizens, responsible for the welfare of their fellow man and woman rather than simply looking out for number one.

My friend Glennon Melton has created a wonderful tribe on her website, *Momastery*, where she published a letter to her son at the start of his third-grade year. It has been shared hundreds of thousands of times. Here is an excerpt:

> *When we seek opportunities to make the world smaller for our kids, it helps them recognize themselves as global citizens, responsible for the welfare of their fellow man and woman rather than simply looking out for number one.*

Chase, we do not care if you are the smartest or fastest or coolest or funniest. There will be lots of contests at school, and we don't care if you win a single one of them. We don't care if you get straight As. We don't care if the girls think you're cute or whether you're picked first or last for kickball at recess. We don't care if you are your teacher's favorite or not. We don't care if you have the best clothes or most Pokémon cards or coolest gadgets. We just don't care.

We don't send you to school to become the best at anything at all. We already love you as much as we possibly could. You do not have to earn our love or pride and you can't lose it. That's done.

We send you to school to practice being brave and kind.

How clearly she spells out to her son their hope that he will recognize the responsibility we each have to show compassion! By letting him know that she and her husband care more about how he shows up as a human being than any contest he might win, they are setting him up to have a sense of authentic self-worth that no outer accomplishment or "attaboys" could ever provide.

Most of us tend to gravitate toward people who are similar to us, but in doing so, we miss out on the opportunities that come from getting to know people who might greatly enrich our lives.

We all know that travel broadens the mind, but you don't need to get on a plane to help your children understand that they are citizens of a world populated by a vast and varied array of fellow humans. Break bread with people from foreign backgrounds, or explore neighborhoods in your city inhabited by people of different cultures. Have a conversation with the taxi driver. Ask your mechanic how he learned his trade. Everyone's life is potentially fascinating if we take time to listen. Everyone has a story to tell. And nothing fosters compassion and generosity like real-life contact with others.

Honoring Our Elders

Until recent times, children grew up around people of every age, from newborns to the aged and infirm. Birth and death were familiar elements of life. Elders were revered. It was a given that you would show respect for those older than you, listening to their stories and seeking out their wisdom.

Today, family members are spread far and wide, and our society relegates old people to facilities where they are largely cared for by strangers.

I find this deplorable. Our society throws away the elderly at inestimable expense. Children need to sit at the feet of their elders. Of course, there are some aged folks who are so miserable that they cannot do much by way of uplifting or guiding others. But most are gold mines of wisdom, insight, and inspiration.

Encounters with those who have lived long and experienced much are priceless. There are remarkable people living in homes for the aged whose bodies may be giving them trouble but whose minds are still sharp. Our children need to be told that their elders were once young, just like them. They, too, danced and partied and fell in love and had their hearts broken. They have wonderful stories to tell.

I have a crop of friends in their eighties and nineties who have greatly enriched my life. Like someone up in a helicopter able to view a wider landscape, elderly folks share wisdom from a much bigger perspective than I have, simply because they have lived more life. The love and support of my elderly friends is invaluable.

Make time to be with grandparents, or adopt an elder or two if you don't have one of your own. Yes, your children may complain or roll their eyes as they are told a story that they've heard ten times already. But in a culture that worships youth and fears aging, valuing our elders helps kids know that getting old is part of life, and not something we turn away from.

As we help our children get to know people outside their immediate circle, they more naturally begin to understand how interdependent we are with our fellow human beings, both those down the street and on the other side of the globe.

> *In a culture that worships youth and fears aging, valuing our elders helps kids know that getting old is part of life, and not something we turn away from.*

Helping Your Kids Make a Difference

From morning till night, kids are told what they can and cannot do, leaving them feeling fairly powerless. For children to become conscious, confident, caring adults, they need to know that they can effect change and that they can make a positive impact on

> For children to become
> conscious, confident, caring
> adults, they need to know that
> they can effect change and that
> they can make a positive impact
> on someone else's life.

someone else's life. What follows are the stories of two children who, empathizing with the tragic plight of children their age living on the other side of the globe, decided to do something. I include their stories not because we should all try to raise children who launch humanitarian movements, but to encourage you to stretch your imagination when you think about helping your children tune in to what stirs them, so they can manifest who they are uniquely meant to be.

Seeing a photograph of two little boys living in slavery prompted eight-year-old Vivienne Harr to do something. She decided she was going to raise money by running a lemonade stand nonstop, for 365 days straight, rain or shine. Her goal was to raise $100,000 to help put an end to child slavery. On day fifty-two, Nicholas Kristof from the *New York Times* showcased Vivienne, and "her moment became a movement." She reached her goal, contributing $101,320 to Not For Sale, a leading anti-slavery organization.

"When her parents said: "You did it, honey. You're done," Vivienne said: "Is child slavery done?" They shook their heads. "Then I am not done." Vivienne, now ten, has catalyzed a movement by starting the organization Make a Stand, "a social impact brand that supports its 10-year-old founder's vision of a world where all 18 million enslaved children are free and safe." When asked, "What advice would you give to kids who have dreams like you but aren't sure they can do it?" Vivienne replied, "If you set your heart to it, you can do it. I promise: you don't have to be big or powerful to change the world. You can be just like me."

Vivienne's parents could have explained to her that while her sentiments were sweet, child slavery was a complicated, grown-up problem. But they didn't. They raised their daughter in a household that valued kindness and concern for others. (Vivienne's mission started because her mother had been deeply touched by photographs of enslaved children at a gallery opening.) From there, they simply buoyed their daughters desire to make a difference.

Free the Children is an international charity that has galvanized more than two million young people to take practical steps toward making the world a better place. It started in 1995 when Craig Kielburger happened on a news article about a young boy in Southeast Asia who had been sold into slavery at the age of four and subsequently spent six years chained to a carpet-weaving loom. Media coverage of Iqbal's story came to the attention of those wanting to silence Iqbal, and he lost his life at the age of twelve for speaking out about the rights of children. When Craig read Iqbal's story, he pulled together a group of his classmates to found Free the Children. He was twelve years old at the time; his classmates were his fellow seventh-graders.

Kids cannot buy a ticket to We Day, an energizing all-day event for teens born out of Free the Children that takes place in fourteen cities; instead, they earn their way through service. Tens of thousands of youth and supporters do so every year. Speakers have included Archbishop Desmond Tutu, Dr. Jane Goodall, Jennifer Hudson, and Magic Johnson. Young people involved with We Act have contributed 14.6 million hours of volunteer service. Long-term studies have found that 80 percent of alumni from these programs volunteer more than 150 hours a year, 83 percent give to charity, and a staggering 79 percent voted in the last Canadian federal election in 2011 (compared to 58 percent overall).

I hope these stories inspire you to look for ways to involve your children in kid-friendly groups like We Day and Make a Stand. So many youngsters suffer from a sense of aimlessness.

They need parents to help them take part in activities that inspire them to step outside their comfort zone and find a sense of purpose, while having fun with their peers. Every child comes into the world with a compassionate nature. Volunteering offers them the chance to experience a sense of meaning when they care for someone else.

Show your children how to give with both hands without asking for anything in return. Involve them in cooking dinner for a housebound neighbor, and let them deliver it. Help out with dog washing at an animal shelter. Participate in park cleanups. Help weed the garden at your local school. Take part in a charity marathon, cheering from the sidelines. You can find many age-appropriate volunteer opportunities at www.volunteermatch.org. Maria Shriver titled one of her blog posts "We're in Need of a Social Kindness Movement." Her moniker? *Scatter kindness.* Please do.

———————•———————

Newsflash: Parenting is really hard.

As I was working on these chapters, describing some of the qualities I believe to be important in helping a child become a confident, compassionate adult, I found myself having a small crisis of faith. Was I crazy to suggest that a parent could embody, let alone teach, all these virtues to their kids? Who can possibly be honest *and* accountable *and* tolerant *and* empathic *and* respectful? Parents are hard enough on themselves as it is; was I only setting them up to feel like failures?

The truth is, parenting is ridiculously difficult because it asks us to manifest qualities in ourselves that we may not yet have given birth to. It demands a level of patience we cannot always locate, especially when we're stretched too thin. Like movies in which the child's character suddenly finds himself in the body of an adult (*Big*), we are often completely unprepared for the responsibility, maturity, and selflessness that come with trying to be our child's role model.

Here is how I resolved that crisis: I realized that it takes unbelievable courage to be a parent. Every day, we wake up and face the possibility of a meltdown over shoes or dirty looks from a snarly teen. It takes courage to be a parent, and there is no elixir or magic pill that makes us brave enough. We simply have to put one foot in front of another and do our best.

My hope is that as you read these chapters, you will just allow the ideas I'm sharing to become seeds in your consciousness. The last thing I want for you is to feel that you've fallen short by not being honest or accountable or compassionate enough.

Simply do your best. Be kind. Make mistakes. Fall down. Get back up. Reach for courage. And if you can't find any, say a prayer or ask a friend to prop you up. It's all one day at a time. Be kind to yourself.

NOW IT'S YOUR TURN

Most humans are innately compassionate; we feel for those who are struggling and wish we could alleviate their suffering. But it is one thing to feel a momentary wave of concern for the plight of those less fortunate, and another to take action.

We're all so busy; when you add children into the mix of an average parent's day, there is hardly time to sit down for a proper meal, let alone organize an outing with our kids to give back to others.

Still, when we stretch our imaginations, we can often find ways to participate with our children in projects that leave us feeling we made a meaningful contribution to the lives of others.

Consider the causes that move you. Some areas include animals, arts, the disabled, seniors, politics, veterans, literacy, the environment, the homeless, and hunger. Think about your children and what need or cause they might be most naturally drawn toward. Or consider what lights *your* fire. Kids often get on board with volunteering because their parent is enthusiastic about a particular cause.

In your journal, write one or two ways you and your kids might dedicate a little time to giving back. It may be assembling Christmas packages for families in need or writing letters to troops overseas. It could be taking the family dog to an assisted-living center, or volunteering to tutor kids with reading problems. The sky really is the limit; you don't need to look further than an elderly neighbor who might love being read to for ways to give back.

MAKING IT PRACTICAL
Parenting with Presence in Real Life

Should my very sensitive son volunteer?

QUESTION: My child feels the pain of others acutely. He is also a worrier. I like to volunteer with him, but he practically falls apart afterward. When we helped feed homeless people over the holidays, he worried that *our* family could end up homeless. When we babysat for a mom at his school who was dealing with chemotherapy, he obsessed about whether *his* mommy would get cancer. I think he does feel very good about helping others, but he gets swept up in their suffering.

SUGGESTION: Oh, these dear, sensitive kids! Their filters are so thin that for them sounds are louder, lights are brighter, and feelings are more intense.

I have worked with many highly sensitive children and consistently find that these kids do best with volunteer opportunities that are less fraught with pain and tragedy. Consider letting your son help out a housebound neighbor by weeding her garden or walking her dog. He might enjoy volunteering to play with little kids at a local nursery school. If your son is a nature lover, he might want to do trail restoration at a local park.

We cannot keep our children in a bubble, nor is it in their best interests. Little by little we need to expose children to some of the complicated and difficult truths about how life is for many of our fellow inhabitants on Earth. But we can be respectful of our child's heightened sensitivity so as to avoid overwhelming him with sorrow and anxiety.

You may find it helpful to take a look at Elaine Aron's book *The Highly Sensitive Child*. Dr. Aron says that in every population — human and animal — about 15 to 20 percent are on the

impulsive end of the spectrum and about 15 to 20 percent are on
the highly sensitive end of the spectrum. Both types are essential
to the survival of the tribe. The impulsive ones push the clan to
explore new territories, while the sensitive souls point out possible dangers that might otherwise be ignored, such as almost
imperceptible scratch marks on a tree, suggesting that bears might
be wandering nearby. Don't give up on looking for ways to let
your little guy make a contribution, but do be sensitive to his sen-
sitivities.

What if we do care about our son's grades?

QUESTION: I like the letter to Chase that you quoted from, but
my wife and I *do* care about whether our son gets As in school or
wins a prize at the science fair. Don't you think it's important to
encourage our children to excel?

SUGGESTION: Absolutely! We all feel good when we know we've
done our best. The problem is, when a child grows up focused
on winning the approval of others, she loses the satisfaction that
comes when she knows in her heart of hearts that she has done
well — even if no one else has noticed.

Ours is a very externally focused, achievement-driven culture. It is true that it's a competitive world, and that kids who have
some degree of drive and persistence do better than those who are
unmotivated. But if children think that we care most about the A
or the honor roll, they may lose sight of the accomplishments that
aren't so easily measured or acknowledged.

I have found that when children learn to be self-referential —
meaning they check in with themselves to see how they feel about
something rather than reflexively looking outside themselves to
determine whether they've done well — they are much stronger at the core. These kids are clearer in their convictions, less

vulnerable to the influence of their peers, and more willing to do the right thing, even if it is unpopular.

Help your children discover the joy of hard work — yes! But let them know that even if there are no prizes, gold stars, or trophies, doing *and being* their best is rewarding in and of itself.

Is it possible to teach kids to like volunteering?

QUESTION: My children don't seem to have any interest in volunteering or helping others. Their school requires them to do community service, but my kids do the quickest, easiest thing possible. They aren't bad kids, but they are very self-centered and they think it's unfair that they have to do even a few hours of giving back each semester. Can you really teach children to feel for others if they don't come by that quality naturally?

SUGGESTION: I have mixed feelings about community-service programs. Overall, I think they are better than nothing, but I agree that you cannot legislate kindness or force someone to feel goodwill toward others. These are internal states of consciousness that arise when we come to understand that we are all passengers in the same boat.

Look for an activity that you can do as a family — one that has some natural appeal. Many kids like animals or feel special when they get to be a big kid around smaller children. Volunteer at a community garden that donates food to shelters, or volunteer to help out at a fundraiser. The more you make helping others *what you do* — perhaps a few hours each month — the less your kids will gripe about it.

Evan, a seventeen-year-old high school senior from Malibu, asked to come in for a session with me. I had worked with him on and off over the years, so it was easy for him to plop down and immediately start speaking truthfully about his struggles. He announced that despite having a great life with more or less everything he wanted, he was depressed. He said he was getting impressive grades, had a terrific girlfriend, was an athletic star, and had been given carte blanche with his father's credit card. And he was depressed.

Evan told me that in one of his classes he had been given the assignment of tallying up his cash outlays for a week. He was stunned to discover that in seven days he had spent more than a thousand dollars. "I realized that my life is all about getting stuff or hanging out with friends or being on my phone so I won't miss anything cool. It's all about me." I asked him what he did that gave him a sense of meaning or purpose. He sat quietly for a while and then responded, "Nothing."

We talked about a variety of ways to address his depression, but he was most eager to explore how he might inject more meaning into his life. By the end of our time together, his mood had lifted considerably. Evan showed real excitement about looking for ways to make his life less about himself, starting with simply being more of an active participant in his family's life instead of just being on the receiving end of his parents' largesse.

I hope you are able to find ways to make the practice of giving to others a regular part of your family's lives in a way that feels enjoyable and gratifying. It really does matter to kids to know that they matter.

CHAPTER 9

Helping Our Kids
Cope with Stress

To sit with a dog on a hillside on a glorious afternoon
is to be back in Eden, where doing nothing
was not boring — it was peace.

— MILAN KUNDERA

For some of us, childhood had a lazy, southern drawl feel to it. Days were spent exploring woods or fields, riding bikes to nowhere in particular, and playing outside until dark. We built towns out of rocks and dirt or converted refrigerator boxes into castles and spaceships. Of course, abuse and neglect were sometimes a sad and secret part of a seemingly idyllic life. But children spent their time differently in the not-so-distant past. We were all in less of a hurry.

Today's kids carry the weight of the world on their backs. They are urged to excel in school, perform impressively in their extracurricular activities, manage complicated relationships (both real and cyber), and compete to get into a good college or find a decent job.

In 2012 it was revealed that 125 Harvard students had been involved in a cheating scandal. Research conducted by the University of Michigan stated that 10 percent of high school sophomores and almost one in eight seniors admitted to using illegally obtained prescription medications ("study drugs") to keep up with their workload. And according to the Journal of Adolescent Health, most teens are getting at least two hours less sleep than is recommended for good health.

In a study titled "Stress in America," commissioned by the American Psychological Association, it was found that 30 percent of teens reported feeling overwhelmed, depressed, or sad as a result of stress. Almost 25 percent said they skipped meals because of stress. Almost one-third of teens say that stress often brings them to the verge of tears. In the past sixty years, the suicide rate has quadrupled for males fifteen to twenty-four years old, and doubled for females of the same age. Suicide rates for those between the ages of ten and fourteen increased more than 50 percent between 1981 and 2006.

Thirty percent of teens reported feeling overwhelmed, depressed, or sad as a result of stress.

The American Academy of Pediatrics released a study noting that stress hormones such as cortisol and adrenaline can have a significant long-term impact on a teen's body, potentially contributing to adult cardiovascular disease, asthma, viral hepatitis, and autoimmune diseases. Stress can unleash chemicals that interfere with the development of neuronal networks in the developing brain as well as inhibit the development of new neurons in growing brains.

The real-life evidence of these statistics regularly shows up in my office. Eight-year-olds whose parents bring them because they have been saying they want to kill themselves. Fourteen-year-olds who use cutting to ease their anxiety and unhappiness. Kids who can't sleep, can't eat, are withdrawn, tearful, or afraid of being alone. I see the bullied and the bullies, the kids who cheat on tests, and those who routinely get drunk to dull the pain and pressure of their lives. It is heartbreaking. Childhood is brief. During this little window of time, our youngsters are meant to explore the world, figure out how to get along with others, discover their gifts, climb, dance, play music...and have fun.

As parents we have a dramatic influence on our children's beliefs about what matters. If we teach them that external achievement is what we care most about, they will naturally look for shortcuts to get ahead — cheating on tests or cutting back on sleep. They need to know that we want them to live with curiosity, excitement, and enthusiasm, and that we are here to *enjoy* life, not to push and shove our way through it.

> *Our kids need to know that we want them to live with curiosity, excitement, and enthusiasm, and that we are here to enjoy life, not to push and shove our way through it.*

When author Geneen Roth interviewed financial advisors, they told her that without exception, every client they worked with who had managed to reach their initial financial goal raised the bar and aimed for something higher. Whatever they had acquired never felt like enough once they had it. They always ended up wanting more.

Connecting in Real Life

A significant contributor to stress is isolation or disconnection. Michael Price, in an interview with Sherry Turkle, author of *Alone Together,* writes, "People today are more connected to one another than ever before in human history, thanks to Internet-based social networking sites and text messaging. But they're also more lonely and distant from one another in their unplugged lives. This is not only changing the way we interact online, it's straining our personal relationships, as well." Turkle tells Price, "When teens tell me that they'd rather text than talk, they are expressing another aspect of the new psychological affordances of the new technology — the possibility of our hiding from each other. They say a phone call reveals too much, that actual conversations don't give them enough control over what they want to say."

Kids step out of school to see their parents looking down at their smartphones. Boys who once chatted with dad between plays as they watched sports now wait while he checks his email instead. Little ones are nursed or bottle-fed while mommy texts, diluting the emotional exchange of this primal, intimate contact. In addition, if mom gets a message that generates anxiety, her tense feelings are communicated to the baby, who experiences them as stress in his relationship with mommy rather than because of outside influences.

In her book *Thrive*, Arianna Huffington shared the following story: "The last time my mother got angry with me before she died was when she saw me reading my email and talking to my children at the same time. 'I abhor multitasking,' she said, in a Greek accent that puts mine to shame. In other words, being connected in a shallow way to the entire world can prevent us from being deeply connected to those closest to us — including ourselves. And that is where wisdom is found."

Connection helps to prevent stress. Nothing fortifies a child like genuine connection with a loved one. In my previous book, I detailed the six stages of attachment that children move through in the first six years of their life, as described by Dr. Gordon Neufeld. We can deepen our attachment with our children throughout their lives with these six inroads, providing our child with one of life's most effective antidotes to stress: healthy connection.

Nothing fortifies a child like genuine connection with a loved one.

The newborn begins its journey of attachment through *proximity*, connecting with us through smell, touch, and the sound

of our voice. At around two, our toddler wants to be like us —
this stage is *sameness* and contributes to a child's acquisition of
language. The next stage is *belonging* or *loyalty* and sees the three-
year-old pushing a sibling off mommy's lap, possessively declaring, "*My* mommy!" When our child is around the age of four, we
strengthen attachment as we acknowledge and celebrate who our
child uniquely is during the stage called *significance*. Connection
goes deeper around five, through the stage of *love* when children
begin to offer us their little hearts. And if all has gone well, from
six on up, we build on a solid foundation of attachment through
the stage of *being known*. We make it clear to our child that we are
capable of hearing her truth, providing support as that calm Captain of the ship, regardless of the storm
she may be sailing through.

Children who have durable, reliable attachments with healthy loved
ones are much better able to cope with
life's stressors. Author Johann Hari
cites research suggesting addiction is a
result of disconnection, not just chem-

> *Children who have durable,
> reliable attachments with
> healthy loved ones are much
> better able to cope with life's
> stressors.*

istry. "If we can't connect with each other, we will connect with
anything we can find — the whirr of a roulette wheel or the prick
of a syringe." He quotes professor Peter Cohen, who says, "We
should stop talking about 'addiction' altogether, and instead call
it 'bonding.' A heroin addict has bonded with heroin because she
couldn't bond as fully with anything else." Hari goes on to say
that "the opposite of addiction is not sobriety. It is human connection."

There will always be youngsters who have close relationships
with their parents but who still struggle mightily with adversity, but generally speaking, attachment with a loving parent

or caregiver offers children a huge advantage in mitigating the stresses of life.

Managing Change and Uncertainty

One of life's greatest certainties is uncertainty. The more we can make peace with the fact that some things are outside our control, the less helpless we will feel when life isn't going according to plan. Demonstrating that we can be flexible in unexpected situations helps our children know that they, too, can tolerate being in limbo while they wait for more to be revealed.

> *Demonstrating that we can be flexible in unexpected situations helps our children know that they, too, can tolerate being in limbo while they wait for more to be revealed.*

I remember once sitting in an airport in Nairobi with my then fifteen-year-old son. It was midnight, and we had just been told that we would not be allowed to board our flight for Australia because the airline did not recognize our electronic visas. Ari started to get nervous; we had no contacts in Nairobi, had been up for nearly twenty-four hours traveling from Tanzania, and departure time was fast approaching. As concerned as I was, I tried to stay relaxed, knowing that how I dealt with the situation was likely to influence how my son handled similar events later on in his life.

I suggested that we make friends with the worst-case scenario. We started talking about things we could do if we were waylaid, reminding ourselves that even if we had to wait in Nairobi a day or two for a traditional visa to come through, we would be okay.

Moments before our flight was ready to depart, the airline received a fax from the Australian consulate, and we were permitted to board. But by then we were confident that if we didn't make our flight, we would simply have a different few days than we'd planned, and that we would be okay.

But helping our children isn't just about teaching them how to cope when things aren't going well. It is also about infusing their days with enjoyment.

Having Fun

It is said that the average four-year-old laughs three hundred times a day; a forty-year-old, only four. In his landmark book *Anatomy of an Illness*, Norman Cousins described how watching just ten minutes of Marx Brothers movies reduced the pain and inflammation from his arthritis and gave him hours of pain-free sleep.

Laughter reduces stress hormones, boosts endorphins, improves the flow of blood to the heart, increases the number of natural virus-killing cells, and makes us more resistant to disease. It improves our mood and attitude, and solidifies bonds between people.

Laughter and fun are wonderful ways to combat stress. Anne Lamott says, "Laughter is carbonated holiness." Music can also be a terrific way of getting out of our heads and into our hearts. Try playing "Oh What a Beautiful Morning" when you're waking the kids in the morning, or Pharrell Williams's "Happy" as you all dance your way to dinner. A small change of state can make a big impact. In chapter 11 you'll find ideas for adding more fun and laughter to your daily life.

Our attitudes about life can make or break our children's stress levels. It isn't always easy to know when we should encourage them to forge through obstacles, and when to teach them that it's okay to let go and chalk up something as a life lesson. But as with every aspect of parenting, how we navigate the twists and turns in *our* lives will influence how our children handle their own.

Persisting

Motivating our children to keep trying when success eludes them is invaluable. It is vital that they develop the inner resources to push through stumbling blocks when it would be easier to throw in the towel. But there is a difference between pursuing dreams with passion and joy and trying to force something to happen when it isn't meant to be. Our kids need to understand that when they don't attain a hoped-for goal, they can try another approach, take a pause in their pursuit, or let go. Not manifesting a particular outcome is not failure, and failure is not fatal. Stumbling along, tripping, and falling is often how we get to where we're going.

> *Stumbling along, tripping, and falling is often how we get to where we're going.*

Let your kids understand that although we might have preferences, we can be at peace when life doesn't go the way we had planned. How does your child see you react to the news that you've missed your flight? Do you look for someone to blame? What do they watch you do when you are told that your car needs a major repair? Do you curse and stomp your feet? Make it evident that when something unexpected happens, you can roll with it. Let them hear you asking the question, "Will this be an issue in five years — or two days?" By letting your children see you putting those bumps in the road into a larger context, they will be inclined to do the same. But if you think that to be okay a situation must unfold exactly as you think it should, you will feel powerless. And powerlessness leads to stress.

There are some who believe that we coddle our children far too much, insulating them from the inevitable bumps and bruises of life by doing everything for them. A story ran a few years ago about a college student who, instead of calling 911 when she discovered a fire in her dorm, called her mother to ask her what she should do. And certainly there is much to say about the helicopter parent who hovers anxiously over her child to make sure every answer on her math sheet is correct or who calls the mother of a friend to "correct an oversight" because her daughter wasn't invited to a birthday party. But there is a difference between coddling and nurturing. Coddling is a manifestation of our own anxiety; we micromanage our child's experiences in the hopes that we will not have to see them distressed or unhappy. Nurturing is an act of love — it involves connecting and being lovingly attuned with our child.

The pressures that kids face today are exceptional, and as stress levels continue to climb, we need to help our youngsters develop good coping strategies.

Paying Attention to Your Child's Stress

If you have a child who is exhibiting ongoing signs of stress or its cousins — anxiety and depression — please don't look the other way. Make sure your kids know that *whatever* they are going through, they can tell you the truth. In my online workshops and trainings I devote a significant amount of time to working with parents so that they don't send their kids a mixed message: *You can tell me anything. Wait a minute — you did* what?! *You're in big trouble!*

Our kids will test us to see if we mean it when we say we want them to come to us if they're feeling worried or stressed, leaking out little grievances to see if we are indeed capable of hearing what's going on with them. Will we be that confident, calm Captain of the ship, or will we leap overboard when our children reveal something that troubles them?

> *If we are to help our kids manage stress and restore their equilibrium when life feels hard, we need to do our own work so that we can honestly tell them, "Whatever you're going through, sweetheart, I'm here and I will help you through this."*

If we are to help our kids manage stress and restore their equilibrium when life feels hard, we need to do our own work so that we can honestly tell them, "Whatever you're going through, sweetheart, I'm here and I will help you through this."

Practicing Mindfulness

"When my sister wore my favorite sweater, I tore up her homework. I was *so mad!*" — Caroline

"My mind tells me things that make me worry, like I'm going to mess up on my oral report and then everybody will laugh at me. I can't stop my thoughts." — David

"I saw a picture online of my friends at a sleepover that I hadn't been invited to. I ended up cutting my leg, I felt so left out and sad." — Tiffany

"I felt really bad when I didn't get the highest score in my class. When I got in my mom's car, I started yelling at her, and then I started crying." — Henry

By now it should be clear that adults aren't the only ones who experience chronic and serious stress. Teens and even young children benefit greatly from learning strategies to help them cope when life isn't going their way. From improving emotional regulation to managing impulsivity, teaching kids how to slow down and reconnect to the present moment gives them an enormous leg up in terms of leading a happier life, both now and into adulthood.

Margaret was a teacher at a school that had implemented a program allowing every student to learn a mindfulness practice. Watching how positively it affected her third-grade students, she decided to try it out with her seven-year-old son, who had recently been diagnosed with ADHD. "I bought a meditation bell and before bed, we closed our eyes, rang the bell, and listened as it faded, while we imagined ourselves floating on a cloud. Sometimes, if he gets really mad at his brother, I hear him ringing that bell upstairs to calm himself down!" She went on to tell me that, like her classroom students, her son was more focused and less fidgety. "Mindfulness practice takes just minutes, and it is really making a difference for these kids."

The term *mindfulness* has gained traction across ages, gender, and demographics. Simply put, it involves paying attention to what is going on in the present moment with curiosity and nonjudgmental awareness. Eckhart Tolle prefers to use the term *presence:* "Mindful seems to imply that the mind is full when the opposite is actually the case." Others use words such as *heartful* or *heightened awareness*. For the purposes of this book, I will use the word *mindful* to represent the quiet, nonthinking awareness that allows us to rest deeply below the surface of whatever external events are creating agitation or stress. These practices involve using senses — sound, feeling, breath — to anchor to the present moment rather than becoming lost in thoughts about the past or future.

> *Mindfulness involves paying attention to what is going on in the present moment with curiosity and nonjudgmental awareness.*

Mindfulness helps children pause before reacting to a stressful situation and to handle difficulties more flexibly. It empowers kids to be less reactive to their thoughts, teaching them that thoughts are just thoughts and, just like the sky is so spacious that it is unperturbed by the presence of clouds, we don't have to be dragged down by every thought-cloud that passes through our awareness. Thoughts come, they stay awhile, and then they disperse.

One way that mindfulness teachers illustrate this idea to children is by filling a jar with water and sand or baking soda, putting on the lid, and then having the children shake up the jar to watch the "storm." When the ingredients settle down, they see that the sand or baking soda has settled to the bottom and the water is clear again. This is very much what happens with our minds. When we get quiet for a few moments, the storm of our thoughts settles down, and we can think and act more consciously.

In families and schools where mindfulness is being taught, children manage their frustration more successfully. In addition, children tend to be more compassionate, cooperative, and patient. Children who were restless learn to be more comfortable in their skin. Kids plagued by anxiety discover that despite their tendency to worry over real or imagined threats, in the present moment, there is no danger. This helps thém reestablish emotional equilibrium when they might otherwise fall apart.

Mindfulness is being introduced in every type of setting, with tremendous results. Former LA Lakers basketball coach Phil Jackson won eleven NBA championships, crediting his wins in part to his use of mindfulness practices. He used to have his players sit in stillness to build their mental strength, and even had Silence Days during which there was no speaking at all. When a player was having a tough time on the court, he could regroup with a mindfulness practice on the bench. Congressman Tim Ryan and others have instituted mindfulness programs for veterans, resulting in a notable reduction in PTSD symptoms. Prisons have started using mindfulness to heal and transform lives, prevent crime, and reduce recidivism.

More than six thousand staff, three thousand parents, and forty thousand students have gone through Linda Lantieri's Inner Resilience Program. She developed this program as a way to help New York City teachers cope with trauma and burnout after 9/11 by introducing meditation, yoga, and time for inner work and reflection. "Because all of those steps we take for outer-preparedness could fall apart. But what we have inside us is not going to break down. We have it in us no matter what."

I have had great success introducing children and their

parents to simple mindfulness practices. A side benefit is the way everyone becomes a little more heart centered.

One day I was in the middle of a particularly difficult session with a mother and her fifteen-year-old daughter. Mom was trying to lay down the law around a house rule that her daughter had broken, and her daughter was radiating malevolence and anger. I asked them, "Would you two mind if we took a break in this conversation and hit the Reset button?" Both agreed; the tension in the room was thick, and we all needed a pause.

I invited them to close their eyes and proceeded to walk them through a short mindfulness exercise. First I asked them to pay attention to their breath, noticing where they sensed it — perhaps in their nostrils as the air flowed past, or at the back of their throat, or maybe in the rising and falling of their chest or stomach. After a moment of this, I asked them to pay attention to whatever sounds they were hearing. "It might be the wind in the trees, or perhaps you'll hear a car driving down the road. You may notice the ticking of a clock, or just the sound of your breath. If your attention wanders, gently bring it back to registering the sounds around you."

We did this exercise for about three minutes. As we wound down, I suggested that they sit quietly for a moment with their eyes closed, allowing their eyes to open when they were ready.

As soon as we looked at one another, I knew things had changed. Both reported feeling much more centered and calm — surprisingly so, after just a few short minutes. The temperature in the room, emotionally speaking, had cooled way down. As we resumed our discussion, there was more openness and less rigidity around their respective positions.

I've done this exercise with six-year-olds and sixty-year-olds and consistently find that simply stopping and tuning in to sounds or sensations or following the breath can bring people back to themselves in a way that just telling them to relax or settle down cannot.

Having a practice that you do with your children each day — ideally in the same place and around the same time — can become a ritual that benefits everyone in the family. Most mindfulness activities are kid friendly and very easy to implement. I have included some of my favorites in chapter 11.

Connection, Connection, Connection

In *And There Was Light*, Jacques Lusseyran writes of the challenges of his life, starting with sudden childhood blindness and including his creation of a French resistance movement and later, surviving life in a concentration camp. "My parents were protection, confidence, warmth. When I think of my childhood I still feel the sense of warmth above me, behind and around me...I passed between dangers and fears as light passes through a mirror. That was the joy of my childhood, the magic armor which, once put on, protects for a lifetime."

The loving bond we form with our children truly can create a touchstone of protection for them, forever.

NOW IT'S YOUR TURN

Can your children tell you the truth? Most of us like to believe that our kids will come to us when they have difficulties. But we often make it hard for our youngsters to offload their upsets, teaching them by our reactivity that it isn't safe to reveal the truth about what they're going through.

If a child tells us that he was caught cheating on a test, or our fourteen-year-old reveals that she is thinking of having sex with her boyfriend, we may find ourselves shouting, threatening, or advising, demonstrating that in fact we really *can't* handle the truth about some of the things our kids are struggling with.

Reflect on how you respond when your child tells you something you don't want to hear. Are you calm and open-minded? Do you get angry or start giving advice? Do you try to fix things rather than letting your youngster off-load whatever she's feeling? Do you punish or bully? Do you effectively shut down the conversation, leaving your child feeling that the next time she is facing a stressful situation she should discuss it with her friends instead of with you?

It isn't always easy, but helping our kids know they can turn to us for support goes a long way toward helping them sail through whatever stormy seas might be creating stress in their lives.

In your journal, write about how safe you make it for your child to come to you when he is stressed about something. By becoming more aware and committing to being more of that calm Captain, you will be better able to stay present with your youngster when stress becomes an issue.

MAKING IT PRACTICAL
Parenting with Presence in Real Life

How can I help my teen if he shuts us out?

QUESTION: My sixteen-year-old has been retreating from the family ever since his first girlfriend broke up with him. I knew he was crushed and tried to tell him it was for the best and that he would find someone else, but he completely shut me out. I feel terrible hearing you talk about the importance of attachment in helping children through stress, because we are so disconnected. How can we help him if he has completely withdrawn from us?

SUGGESTION: As I said earlier, we teach our children whether or not it is safe to reveal what's going on in their lives by how we respond when they open up to us. When we react with advice or appear desperately unhappy about their unhappiness, they learn to guard their secrets lest they risk having not only to handle *their* stress but also the pressure of *our* upset about *their* problems.

Rebuilding connection takes patience and time, but it can be done. While your sixteen-year-old is at a stage when kids pull away to separate from their parents, this does not mean your son doesn't need you. However, if you come *at* him with the aroma of neediness — desperate to know the details of his life or tripping over yourself to restore his happiness — he will instinctively retreat.

Look for small, less intrusive opportunities to connect. Perhaps your son will be interested in helping you whip up a new dessert. Or maybe you can ask him to share some great music he's recently discovered. If he *does* reveal something about a challenge he's dealing with — however small or innocuous — try to respond with interest without delivering a barrage of questions or unleashing a torrent of advice.

For more on attachment, please see chapter 9, or learn more about the online in-depth programs I offer at SusanStiffelman .com.

What can I do when my daughter gets stressed by what happens in her online world?

QUESTION: My daughter is fourteen and gets stressed out by things that happen between her friends online. When I try to convince her to stay out of upsetting arguments, she says I don't understand. She ends up losing sleep sometimes because of hurtful posts directed either at her or at one of her friends.

SUGGESTION: It is almost impossible for kids to navigate the social complexities of their online world. In a sense, it is uncharted territory for parents as well. How do we set boundaries or provide just the right amount of supervision so that our youngsters enjoy what goes on in Cyberville without becoming confused, hurt, or even tormented?

Let your daughter know that you agree — you can't know how much is at stake for her when it comes to her online friendships but that you want to help her be less affected when things start turning ugly. Instead of giving her advice she isn't asking for (I call this *crashing the party*), ask your daughter to explain how you can best help her; let her tell you what kind of support she needs when she's struggling. If she just wants to unload, let her do that. If she learns that you can listen without becoming preachy, she is more likely to let you weigh in with your counsel.

If you manage to build her trust enough that she lets down her guard, proceed with caution. Demonstrate curiosity. "You seem so mad when people make fun of something you've posted. Can you help me understand what makes you want to keep checking your page when you're pretty sure there are just going to be hurtful comments?" Or, "Sweetheart, I wonder if it helps Cassie when you start defending her by posting mean things to kids when they attack her, or whether it would mean more to her if you unplugged your computer and just called her up to see how she's doing."

I think all parents are flying by the seat of their pants when it comes to helping kids navigate the digital world. It starts with being sensible. If your daughter was spending time at a local hangout and consistently came home bruised or crying, you would address the problem at its root rather than just forbidding her to set foot outside the house. Help her feel you are her ally rather than an outside controlling force only interested in limiting her fun.

How can I help my son the perfectionist?

QUESTION: How do you help kids know when they should try their hardest and when they should let go? As glad as I am that my twelve-year-old son tries his best, I sometimes wish he wouldn't insist on trying to make his assignments perfect. He obsesses over every detail. My wife and I worry about how he's going to handle high school if he gets this stressed over sixth-grade homework.

SUGGESTION: Some children seem to have been born with a perfectionistic streak. Try as we might, it is hard to convince them to lighten up about things that matter to them. But many kids seem to mimic one or both parents' need for perfection, internalizing the idea that good has to be great, and great has to be fantabulous.

Tell your son that you would like to understand what it's like when the voice in his head pushes him on, even when he is tired or burnt out. "What is that like for you, to know that you've done a terrific job and you still feel unsatisfied?" When you demonstrate that you want to visit his planet and get a better feel for what he's up against — without judging or criticizing him — he may become more open and, eventually, more receptive to your guidance.

It could also be that your son is something of an "approval junkie," clamoring for attention or praise from his teachers. If this is the case, look at what he gains from special approval that he might be able to get in another way. There is nothing wrong with wanting to impress a teacher with a job well done, but if it is causing undue stress, the underlying need is best addressed in another way.

If you feel your son is taking his perfectionistic cues from you or your wife, make a point of modeling more balance. When you're working on a project, let him see you acknowledging that although you could probably make it better, good enough is good enough. Take a break, call it a day, and let go. Hopefully, he'll get the message that while it's commendable to do things well, nothing is worth sacrificing our health or well-being over.

CHAPTER 10

Happiness Is
an Inside Job

Piglet noticed that even though he had a very small heart,
it could hold a rather large amount of Gratitude.

— A. A. MILNE

When I was a teenager in the 1970s, I once wandered into a New Age bookshop in Kansas City and picked up a little blue book called *Discourses of Meher Baba*. I actually had no idea what a discourse was, but the first line stayed with me for the rest of my life: "Say, 'I do not want anything' and be happy." As young and inexperienced as I was, this idea resonated all the way down to my bones; I knew it was true, even if I wasn't entirely sure I understood what it meant or how to go about embodying it.

Countless luminaries have said the same thing — that the key to happiness lies in freeing oneself from desire. When we are at peace with life just as it is, we liberate ourselves to experience true joy. I believe that with all my heart.

This does not mean we should raise our children to drift through life without honoring the nudges and longings of their spirit. Yearning is often the language of our deepest self, prompting us to develop our unique talents and gifts. It is a matter

> *When we are at peace with life just as it is, we liberate ourselves to experience true joy.*

of maintaining a balance between what Eckhart Tolle calls *being* and *becoming*. In his lectures, he explains that if we're too focused on *becoming* we lose the ability to enjoy the present moment, falling into patterns of stress, anxiety, and never feeling fulfilled. But if we only stay in a state of *being*, we are not very effective in the world. Eckhart describes this as going *below thought*, explaining that if we abandon all striving, we can actually lose a sense of alertness, which is part of being present. We need to maintain a balance between being and doing for life to be enjoyable and fruitful.

But living in a culture that tempts us with an endless parade of things that promise to make us *really* happy makes maintaining that balance easier said than done. And raising kids who don't desperately want one thing or another? Quite challenging. Our children are bombarded with the promise of popularity, approval, status, or pleasure if they can acquire something that is usually just out of reach. "If I just get an A on that test…If Cameron tells Caitlyn that he *does* like me…If you guys would buy me a newer iPad with a better camera…"

This calls to mind a survey by Pew Research Center in which, when asked what they aspired to be, 81 percent of eighteen- to twenty-five-year-olds responded that what they most wanted to be was rich. It isn't easy to counteract the impact of advertisers that make it seem as though life without x, y, or z just isn't quite up to snuff.

But happiness cannot be bought. In my psychotherapy practice, some of my most despondent clients grace the covers of magazines, own homes all over the world, and live seemingly idyllic lives, frequently photographed frolicking in the Malibu surf with their stunning spouse and picture-perfect kids at their side. Few would guess that they limp through their days depressed and brokenhearted, or that they attempt to manage their unhappiness with drugs or alcohol. Everything looks great from the outside — the shiny red apple — but inside is a worm, eating away at their soul.

As I was leafing through a copy of *Architectural Digest,* featuring impeccably designed houses — dreamy kitchens, showcase living rooms, hand-crafted furniture, and every pillow placed just so — I started thinking about the families living in these homes. Certainly some of the residents move through the sumptuous rooms in appreciation and delight. But I have known people who spent years manifesting their dream home and ended up facing the painful truth that happiness is not for sale; heartache still seeped in. Maybe the family *doesn't* gather around the massive stone fireplace in the cathedral-ceilinged imported oak–beamed living room to share laughs and play games in the evenings. Maybe the kids routinely sulk in their designer bedrooms, miserably consumed with trying to impress their online friends. The house might be worthy of envy, but not the lives being lived within its walls.

There is nothing wrong with enjoying the finer things in life, and many wealthy people live gratifying lives filled with love, joy and purpose. I just want to highlight that worldly success and happiness do not go hand in hand. The elements that contribute to a fulfilling life go far beyond what money can buy.

Making Peace with Not Getting All We Want

When we understand that happiness is not something we can buy, we become more at ease with our children's complaints when they can't have something they want. But rather than criticizing them for not being grateful enough, we should help them navigate through their disappointment, validating their feelings and guiding them toward acceptance.

I remember one awful day when my then eight-year-old son cried all the way home because I wouldn't buy him a thirty-dollar

Pokémon card. Oh, how he wanted that card! It would have been so easy to buy his smile. But we had set a dollar limit, and the card far exceeded it. I felt terrible. He wanted it so much. What would be the harm in giving in?

But I wanted him to know that I had faith in his ability to weather the storm of not getting what he wanted. I tried to be kind and understanding; "I know how badly you want it, sweetheart. I know it doesn't seem fair." But somehow I held my ground. As hard as it was, I believe *not* getting what he wanted helped him learn that his happiness wasn't dependent on mommy pulling out her credit card.

As I said, wanting is not in and of itself a negative thing. Desire and longing are often whispers from our soul, indicating the direction we should take in our life. Why would an athlete spend grueling days working out and perfecting his ability if he didn't long to be his best? How would I have learned Hindi if I had ignored my desire to do so? It is only when pining for something sucks the oxygen out of today by promising us a better tomorrow that it becomes a problem.

Help your children learn the difference between the monkey mind's endless demands for "stuff" and the genuine yearnings of their soul. It is a gift to be attuned to the call of the heart. The trick is in not putting all the eggs in the basket of "Someday, I'll be happy, if and only if..." The journey *is* the destination, even when we aspire to great heights. We are meant to not only reach for the stars, but to enjoy the ride.

We are meant to not only reach for the stars, but to enjoy the ride.

When the atmosphere in our home is loving and light, when we instill within our kids a sense of purpose, when we give back to others, and when we help them stay lovingly connected to themselves and others, we provide our youngsters with the ingredients for an exceptionally good life.

Helping our children live more joyful lives also requires that we teach them to challenge negative habits and thinking patterns — changing our happiness set point, or our default capacity for feeling joy.

Changing Our Happiness Set Point

Researchers in positive psychology believe that we have a happiness "set point" — a subjective level of well-being that stays relatively constant. Lottery winners tend to revert back to their happiness set point even after winning millions of dollars, as do those who have suffered a great loss. My friend Marci Shimoff says that this set point is determined by three things: genetics (50 percent), habits (40 percent), and circumstances (10 percent.)

At first glance, this might suggest that if you were unfortunate in the genetic lottery and inherited genes biased toward "glass half empty," there is a 50 percent chance that you will be destined to live an unhappy life. But such is not the case. Epigeneticists have determined that changing our habits can actually change our DNA. Dr. David Rakel states: "Epigenetics means 'around the gene' or if you will, the soup in which we bathe our genes is determined by human choice.... We have a choice to bathe our genes with joy, happiness, exercise, and nutritious foods, or we can bathe them with anger, lack of hope, junk food and sedentary lifestyle." In other words, regardless of our circumstances or genetics, we can cultivate happiness.

It is said that we think about sixty thousand thoughts each day. It is also said that about 80 percent of them are negative. And it is believed that about 95 percent of the thoughts we think today are more or less the same ones that we thought yesterday, the day before, and the day before that. This means that if we don't change

> *If we don't change our habitual way of thinking, we will be drenched in about forty-five thousand negative thoughts each and every day.*

our habitual way of thinking, we will be drenched in about forty-five thousand negative thoughts each and every day. That's a pretty negative soup for our genes to be swimming around in!

When NIH researchers measured blood flow and activity patterns in the brain, they discovered that negative thoughts stimulate areas involved in anxiety and depression, acting like a poison on our system. The best way to help our kids develop healthy habits of happiness is to adopt them ourselves.

Do your children see you falling into a negative "what if" spiral when life deals you a difficult hand, or do you try to whistle a happy tune as you do your best to make lemonade out of lemons? Naturally, you may *prefer* that your car transmission doesn't break down or that the rain lets up before your outdoor party. But there is a difference between preferences and needs. When we *need* something, we step into a place of powerlessness, fueling desperation and the unhealthy behaviors that come with trying to control a particular outcome because we cannot imagine enduring the alternative.

When our children see us acknowledging disappointment without flinging ourselves headlong into unhappiness, they develop a picture of what it looks like to remain present through life's rough patches — a way of being that they can refer back to when they encounter their own challenges.

Reaching within for Happiness

When some of us think of happiness, we picture a quarterback doing the happy dance after making a touchdown, or a bride beaming with delight as she walks down the aisle. These moments are indeed special, but they are relatively few and far between. They are also dependent on external circumstances.

True happiness is quiet and deep. It is not dependent on circumstance. It isn't something we get by manifesting a longed-for event or achievement. Instead, it is a state we settle into that infuses the moments of our life — ordinary and extraordinary alike — with deep joy.

> *True happiness is quiet and deep. It is a state we settle into that infuses the moments of our life — ordinary and extraordinary alike — with deep joy.*

Author Barbara De Angelis tells a personal story that made quite an impact on me. I'd like to paraphrase it here. After years of searching, she met a man she believed to be her soul mate. They fell deeply in love, and she marveled at her good fortune. As they walked hand in hand on the beach, Barbara's heart overflowed with happiness. Her sweetheart sent her passionate love letters. She moved through her days saturated in a kind of romantic bliss she had never known.

Some months later, she discovered that this man was actually seeing several other women. Adding insult to injury, he had sent them the same love letters he had written to her. She was shattered. How could a love that had felt so true and deep have been a sham? Brokenhearted, she shut off the world and plunged into a deep, dark hole.

After some time in this dismal condition, something shook loose inside of her, and she had an epiphany. If her entire experience of love had been based on a falsehood, why had she felt so much happiness? She began to understand that the joy and love she had experienced in this man's presence, and whenever she thought about him, *had been inside her* all the time. He didn't hand her a chunk of love whenever they were together. He didn't give her a pill that opened the floodgates of her heart. Instead, his expressions of affection had simply prompted her to turn on the faucet of joy within herself. It was *her* opening the faucet that allowed her to experience magnificent love, not something he did.

In truth, her boyfriend had simply been the excuse she needed to allow herself to experience feelings of love that always had been in her heart.

What I love about this story is the way it exposes a lie that many of us perpetuate: that our happiness is dependent on something or someone else. When you reflect on times when you have been steeped in joy, you may first remember what was going on externally; perhaps your loved ones were all gathered together, or you were taking a walk in the woods.

But while those conditions are important, the *feeling* of happiness was humming within you. True happiness is self-generated; it is a feeling we can tap into regardless of what is going on externally. What a wonderful gift it would be if we could help our children understand that happiness really is an inside job!

When we open our hearts to appreciate whatever the present moment is delivering, then reaching for a piece of bread can catalyze as much happiness as reviewing a list of things that we are grateful for — an essential lesson to teach our kids.

When we open our hearts to appreciate whatever the present moment is delivering, reaching for a piece of bread can catalyze as much happiness as reviewing a list of things that we are grateful for — an essential lesson to teach our kids.

There is an ever-present river flowing inside of us that we can always step into. Real happiness is about enjoying the simple miracle of being alive.

Expressing Appreciation

Appreciation is not something we can teach our children through words, but if we create *habits* of gratitude, they cannot help but be affected. Expressing appreciation regularly helps us shift away from fixating on what's wrong to celebrating what is wonderful.

John Gottman is a professor of psychology and the author of many books, including *The Seven Principles for Making Marriage Work*. In the course of his research on marital stability, he came up with a technique that is useful not only in marriages but also in other family relationships: establishing a ratio of five appreciations to every one negative comment.

He suggests that whenever you make a complaint, you should neutralize its impact with five positive acknowledgments or appreciations. Harville Hendrix, creator with his wife of Imago Relationship Therapy, talks about this idea as well, encouraging couples to shift from patterns of communication that harm to ones that uplift. I have had great success working with families to integrate this idea into their daily lives; children (and parents!) love hearing the things we like or appreciate about them. If, out of frustration, you find yourself saying something like, "Why do you always make so much noise when you eat?" you can sprinkle positive comments throughout the day, such as, "I loved how gently you played with the puppies, sweetheart" or "When I pulled into the driveway and saw you playing outside, I was so happy to see you, and so glad to be your dad!" Offering appreciations to those we love is like lubricating an engine; it reduces friction and makes family life run more smoothly.

Answering Your Child's Big Questions about Life

The words *spiritual* and *spirituality* carry a multitude of meanings. Here I am using them not in a religious or dogmatic sense but to describe the longing we are born with to understand how we came to be alive, what power or force (if any) is running the show, and why we are here in the first place. We human beings seem to come with a preprogrammed yearning to understand the mystery of life. We look beyond rational explanations for a deeper frame-work for understanding the universe, and our place in it.

Your personal view of spirituality may include a belief in God or a benevolent force governing the universe. It may be some-thing you associate with angels or spirit guides, or the traditions of indigenous people who have long inhabited this Earth. Your beliefs may have been defined by your parents or the community in which you grew up. Or you may have rejected those beliefs, embracing something far different that resonates more closely with your heart and sensibilities.

Regardless of our practices or beliefs, we need to think about how we want to convey them to our children. Do we want them to go to Sunday school? Are there certain rituals we want to incor-porate into their day? Do we want them to learn passages from scripture? Will we pray before meals or bedtime? Do we believe they should be exposed to a variety of religions, so they can make their own choices? Are we atheist or agnostic, determined not to infuse our youngsters with any particular beliefs so they can find their own way?

These are very personal decisions, ones I trust parents to sort out for themselves. But we need to be prepared with at least some basic answers once our children begin to ask the big questions about life, including what happens when a loved one passes on.

In the movie *Cocoon*, there is a scene that resonates deeply for me. In it (spoiler alert), a young woman undresses in her cabin and, rather than just removing her clothes (which the fellow peer-ing through a peephole hopes she is about to do), she removes her skin — entirely, from head to toe. Underneath, she is a lumi-nous being of brilliant light. The fellow peeping from next door is rendered dumbstruck. She simply removes her outer identity to become who she really is — a pure being of light.

I love this image and sometimes bring it to mind it as I am

moving through my day. As I interact with people, I imagine that beneath their outward persona, they — like me — are just manifestations of divinity, poured into the tube of a body to play and learn here on earth for a time. Sometimes I even imagine that each person I meet is God or the divine presence in disguise — both of us knowing we aren't the part we are playing, while (hopefully) having lots of fun playing it out anyway.

This idea may be of no use to you, but with some children it can be helpful to explain that our spirit is something akin to light that is poured into the container of our body, and that this is why when someone dies, the love and connection that we feel for them remains. Again, I trust that each parent will find the right way to talk about life and death with his or her own child. For some, that may mean saying nothing at all. Their approach may be to quietly lead a compassionate life, allowing their children to absorb what it is to walk a spiritual path by living it themselves.

But some parents may be quite passionate about their spiritual practice. They may faithfully attend church, meditate daily, listen regularly to lectures by inspiring spiritual teachers, bow at the altar of their guru every morning, commune with their angels or spirit guides, or go on retreats to deepen their faith. *Sometimes* the children of these passionate devotees find their parents' spiritual pursuits absurd and want no part of them. Like the Michael J. Fox character on *Family Ties*, who adamantly rejects his parent's liberal mind-set and becomes a teenage suit-and-tie-wearing Republican, our kids may reject our spiritual beliefs, even repudiating them with ridicule and disdain.

> *If the ways that you nourish your soul are real to you, they needn't be validated by anyone — including your children.*

As disappointing as it might be to end up with a child who resists any and all efforts to impart your beliefs, it can also be a blessing. If the ways that you nourish your soul are real to you, they needn't be validated by anyone — including your children. I've seen parents sabotage any hope of getting their kids to embrace their spiritual practices by forcing them to participate in them. It doesn't work that way.

Yes, expose your children to the things that nourish your spirit. But let them come to those practices on their own, by watching how you are made calmer or more loving and generous because of them. Once again, our children can be our greatest teachers. They will sniff out and expose any hypocrisy in us. If we are pushy about what we believe or come across as needing them to join us on our path, they will be repelled. If we come out of our rooms after meditating with a snarly attitude, they will lose respect for whatever inner experience of peace we claim to have soaked ourselves in. If we return from church gossiping about the people we saw there...you get the picture. Our kids insist on keeping it real.

There's no need to emerge from your spiritual practice in a saintly fashion, floating into the room with a beatific smile and speaking in hushed tones as you ask your children if they would mind cleaning up their toys. But be aware that kids learn far more from what they see than from what we say. If you want them to embrace your spiritual path — or at least be open to exploring it — don't shove it down their throats. Let them be drawn, as you were, because of a feeling within them that beckons, while you bring your practice to life in their presence.

> *Let your children be drawn, as you were, because of a feeling within them that beckons, while you carry on quietly living your practice in their presence.*

NOW IT'S YOUR TURN

Below is a list of the qualities I've discussed in the last few chapters. I have covered a lot of territory and no doubt have left out attributes that you may feel are essential in raising your child. Take a moment to reflect on the characteristics *you* believe to be important. In your journal, write a line or two about a specific shift you could make that might help you and your child develop more of that quality.

For example, if you choose "respecting ourselves," you may decide to practice being more assertive with your coworker when he repeatedly asks you to cover for him so he can take a longer lunch. If you've chosen "being accountable," you may set an intention to talk with your kids about ways that each member of your family will handle those inevitable moments when you hurt someone's feelings or disregard their request. If you choose "living with passion and purpose," perhaps you'll do a little research on a place where you and your kids can volunteer. Or you may decide to take a writing class to show your kids what it looks like to pursue the quiet longings of your heart.

As a reminder, here are the qualities we have discussed:

Apologizing
Being accountable for our choices
Being happy and content
Being honest
Being vulnerable
Communicating well
Connecting
Coping with stress
Cultivating compassion
Dealing with anger
Demonstrating good manners

Developing empathy
Enjoying life
Enjoying our own company
Feeling worthy of love
Giving back
Having fun
Honoring our elders
Honoring spirituality
Keeping agreements
Listening respectfully
Listening to our intuition
Living with passion and purpose
Managing uncertainty
Practicing gratitude
Practicing mindfulness
Practicing self-care and kindness
Pruning unhealthy relationships
Resetting our happiness set point
Respecting others
Respecting ourselves
Setting boundaries in relationships
Strengthening attachment
Telling the truth

MAKING IT PRACTICAL
Parenting with Presence in Real Life

Should we make our kids attend church?

QUESTION: My husband and I attend a nondenominational church on Sundays. We have always felt that it was important for our children to come with us, which they did happily when they were younger. But now my fifteen-year-old son says it's stupid, and my thirteen-year-old wants to be like his big brother, so he is also refusing to go. What should we do?

SUGGESTION: There are two schools of thought on how to answer your question. One would suggest that there are many benefits to establishing a weekly practice of devoting time to prayer, contemplation, worship, and thanksgiving. This point of view recognizes that children are not inclined to eagerly to get up on Sundays to go anywhere that isn't "fun" and that parents should be firm in their commitment to involve the family in a regular activity that places focus on nurturing meaningful qualities, even if the kids complain.

The other position suggests that forcing children to place their bodies in a house of worship does little to awaken their natural interest in God or spirituality. Taking it further, a forced presence at Sunday services may actually *dis*incline children from spiritual pursuits because of the negative association they internalize from going through the motions of reverence without having a genuine interest.

I believe that if parents demonstrate genuine enthusiasm about devotion to some form of spiritual activity, they should trust that it matters less that their children show up physically than that they feel the ripples of their parent's joy, peace, and devotion. Ultimately, this is what will most influence a child to explore his or her own spirituality. But every parent has to figure this out for him- or herself. Some will feel — understandably — that showing up, even reluctantly, is better than staying home to sleep in or watch TV.

If your fifteen-year-old wants to take a break from attending your church, perhaps it is wise to let him do so; as the saying goes, you can lead a horse to water, but you can't make him drink. You can certainly *ask* him to join you for what you believe to be a special and valued family ritual, but you may find he's more likely to return if he is allowed to choose rather than because he is forced to attend. If you think your younger son actually enjoys going with you, try talking with him about the importance of thinking for himself and making choices that feel right to him, rather than ones that are motivated by an attempt to win his brother's approval.

Have I spoiled my children?

QUESTION: I have worked like crazy to provide a good life for my family, and sure enough, my kids don't appreciate the expensive furniture or the fancy home we live in. All they care about is getting the latest gadgets or the coolest clothes. Is it too late to teach them to appreciate what they have, instead of complaining about what they don't have? Have I spoiled them forever?

SUGGESTION: I have never been a fan of the term *spoiled* when it comes to describing children. Spoiled milk? Yes. Spoiled children? No. Kids naturally want what they want — often letting us know very forcefully! But we are the ones who teach them to expect to get whatever they ask for. We need to be able to trust in their ability to endure the disappointment of not having every wish fulfilled.

Getting angry at children for being ungrateful because we have suddenly decided to stop buying them everything they desire is a bit unfair. If your family has always chased after whatever is new and shiny, it is unreasonable to expect your youngsters to suddenly fall into a state of perpetual appreciation.

Change your children's experience of daddy love. Start providing them with the things that money can't buy but that truly satisfy: long bike rides, epic Monopoly games, adventures into parts of town you have never explored, or family movie nights. Let them see *you* appreciating the intangibles of life — the pleasure of a good book or the joy of seeing something you've planted in the garden bear fruit. When you change what you value, your children will be more likely to shift out of wanting things and into being grateful for what they have.

It may take time for your kids to let go of the wanting game. Don't blame them for being unappreciative. When they ask for something, invite them to add it to a Special Someday Wish List. Help your children discover the pleasure of working and saving up for things they especially want. Acknowledge their disappointment and frustration with understanding when they are deprived of something (You may want to read about Act I Parenting in chapter 5 or in *Parenting Without Power Struggles* for more on this strategy.)

Can a person go from being negative to positive?

QUESTION: My family tree has depression all over it. Is it really possible to change from being someone who habitually entertains negative thoughts to someone who is positive and hopeful?

SUGGESTION: This is the miracle of our lives: that we can grow up in circumstances that appear to define the trajectory of our life and break free to create something entirely new for ourselves.

Yes, it will be work for you to challenge long-standing patterns of negative thinking. Those patterns are habitual, and habits are not easy to break. It will take commitment and awareness to keep yourself from slipping into the well-worn grooves of viewing unpleasant experiences as inevitable or pushing away the good because you don't trust it to be real.

But you *can* liberate yourself from the constraints of your family tree. You have free will. You can choose how you think about the dance of life, seeing difficult moments as opportunities to grow and lovely ones as gifts from a benevolent universe.

This doesn't mean that you should ignore support if you need it, whether that includes medication, therapy, or lifestyle changes — including diet, sleep, exercise, meditation, or play. But be a trailblazer, break old family patterns, and shatter the glass ceiling of your family's capacity for joy!

CHAPTER 11

Tools, Tips,
and Strategies

*The only thing that is ultimately real about your journey
is the step that you are taking at this moment.
That's all there ever is.*

— ECKHART TOLLE

Much of what I have written about raising children to be conscious, confident, and caring will be familiar. We know it's important to practice an attitude of gratitude and that it's wise to live in the moment. It's the putting-it-into-action part that some of us have trouble with. It is all well and good to *know* that we should be more present with our kids or live in a state of thankfulness. It's an entirely different thing to incorporate that understanding into our day-to-day lives.

Many of us are committed to making the world a better place, often devoting considerable time and energy to our favorite humanitarian causes. But we have a chance right in front of us to positively impact the world. Our parenting path provides us with a practical opportunity to help build a better world by raising children who grow into conscious, caring adults.

In this chapter, I offer you a variety of activities that can be integrated into your daily lives. Some ideas will speak to you; others not so much. But I urge you to weave at least a few of these practices into your life. While I encourage you to do them with your youngsters, all these activities can be done on your own as well.

Practices for Cultivating Mindfulness, Awareness, and Consciousness

"Mom, are you even listening to me?"

"Dad, I told you twice already that I needed a ride."

"You said you just had to check your work email for a minute, and that was a long time ago!"

As I've said several times now, our children can be among our very best teachers, providing us with unlimited opportunities to step into bigger shoes. One of the ways they keep us in check is by pointing out when we have *checked out.*

As mentioned previously, mindfulness practices are breaking loose of meditation centers and making their way into schools, prisons, and hospitals. How wonderful if they could be part of a child's life from early on! Imagine a world in which children grew up being present with their feelings, less at the mercy of stressful thoughts, and with a sense of gratitude humming in the background of their daily lives.

Here, then, are some ideas for bringing mindfulness practices into your family's life. It is always best to lead by example, so if you have never done any form of mindfulness or meditation, I suggest doing so for at least a month before introducing it to your children.

SET THE STAGE

The specifics of how you introduce mindfulness and meditation practices will vary based on your child's age and developmental stage, but in general, you might say something like this: "You may have noticed that I sometimes like to sit quietly and just be still for a little while in the morning (afternoon, evening.) When I do that, I feel really nice and peaceful inside, and it helps me through my day.

"I'd like to teach you how to do that, too. Would you like that?" (It's helpful to get children to "sign up," rather than deciding for them that mindfulness is something they have to do. Most kids will be interested, but it is still a good idea to ask them if they'd like to learn.)

"Mindfulness is really simple. It's just noticing what is going on in this moment instead of thinking about the past or the future. What I like about it is that it helps me feel calmer and happier. The first thing we're going to do is create a special place where we can spend a few minutes practicing it together each day. I thought we could make this area (point out a specific part of your house) that place. Will you help me set it up?" (Invite your children to take part in creating an inviting space, perhaps with cushions, flowers or indoor plants, or little trinkets that have meaning to each of you. If you're comfortable burning a scented candle or incense, the fragrance makes it easier for some to stay anchored in the present.)

Once you have established your mindfulness area, you may begin your first practice.

BEGIN THE PRACTICE

"Let's get nice and comfortable. Let go of tightness and tension, starting at the top of your head and imagining a warm ball of light relaxing all the muscles in your face and jaw, moving down into your neck and shoulders, allowing each muscle to soften as you let go of any feeling of tightness or tension." Continue guiding the child into relaxation, from head to toe.

One of the easiest ways to introduce mindfulness to children is to use a meditation bell or a Tibetan singing bowl. After striking the gong or making the tone, ask your children to listen very carefully as the sound becomes softer and softer. You can suggest that they raise their hand when they can no longer hear the tone. This will focus their attention on the sound and nothing else

Another activity children enjoy is one mentioned in chapter 9. Instruct your children to listen to whatever sounds are around them — indoors or out. Tell them that if they notice their mind wandering — which it will — they can just gently bring it back to whatever noise captures their attention — the sound of a car going by, their tummy growling, a dog barking. Whatever it is, encourage them just to register the sounds around them in a relaxed, effortless way.

FOLLOW THE BREATH

One of the most common mindfulness practices involves following the breath. Say to your children, "As you breathe in, pay attention to the breath coming in. Notice the air as it comes into your nostrils. Is it warm or cool? Follow it to the back of your throat, and as it makes its way into your lungs. For the next moment or so, just pay attention to your breath, in your nose, or the back of your throat, or maybe in the rising and falling of your belly as you breathe in and out, or perhaps in the sound made as you inhale and exhale. If your mind wanders — and it probably will — just come back to noticing your breath." Be quiet for a few breaths so they can continue to do this.

You can also have your child count her inhales and exhales to give her mind something to do as she settles in to riding the ebb and flow of her breath. Tell your child, "Relax your body. When you're ready, take a breath and while inhaling, count 'one, one, one, one, one, one, one.' As you breathe out count 'one, one, one, one' until your lungs are empty. Wait for the next breath — don't rush. Then breathe in, counting two, two, two, and as you exhale, count 'two, two, two, two' until you are empty of air. You may prefer just to count on the inhale or on the exhale; either is fine. Continue this for ten breaths. Notice how it feels to continue breathing without counting for another few moments."

PLACE HANDS ON CHEST AND BELLY

When we exert ourselves or move into a stressful state, we tend to breathe from our chest, and our breaths are more rapid and shallow. When we are relaxed, we breathe more slowly from our belly. A simple but effective way to regain a sense of presence is to invite your child to place one hand on her chest and the other on her belly. "As you breathe in and out, notice which hand is rising and falling. Don't try to make one or the other hand change what it's doing; just pay attention to which hand is moving more." After your child observes her breathing and hands for a while, you can encourage her to shift her breathing to her belly. Afterward, you may ask if she noticed feeling any different when she was breathing from her belly instead of her chest. If she says she felt calmer, suggest that this is something she could do when she's feeling upset, worried, or extra fidgety.

After a mindfulness session, many children enjoy sharing what it was like for them — including the difficulties they may have had staying focused as well as any calm feelings they are experiencing. They might also enjoy hearing how it was for you. Listen openly, and let them know how much you enjoyed that special time together.

OBSERVE EMOTIONS

Mindfulness helps children understand what they are feeling so that they are less at the mercy of the storms of big emotions that, left unchecked, can build into a tsunami.

Have your children sit quietly or lie down with their eyes closed and tune in to what's going on inside them. "Notice how you are feeling: excited, angry, sad, worried, content, curious. You may feel different feelings at the same time — excited *and* a little worried. Don't try to change anything — just notice what you're feeling." When we help them accept their emotions without resistance, our kids become better able to manage their big feelings.

In her book of mindfulness exercises for kids, *Sitting Still Like a Frog*, Eline Snel has children describe their feelings by delivering their Personal Weather Report. Ask them: Are they feeling sunny, stormy, windy, calm, rainy, or in the midst of a hurricane? By tuning into and identifying what they're experiencing, they can create some distance between themselves and their emotions. As Snel describes it, children can recognize, "I am not the downpour, but I notice that it is raining; I am not a scaredy-cat, but I realize that sometimes I have this big scared feeling somewhere near my throat."

LET THOUGHTS BE CLOUDS DRIFTING BY

This is an interesting activity to do with children, especially those who worry a lot. Invite them to sit comfortably, eyes closed, while tuning in to their breath in one of the ways we have discussed. "As you sit, you may notice or hear thoughts passing through your mind. Without trying to make those thoughts go away — which is impossible anyway — just notice them. Pretend that you're the blue sky — so big that a few clouds would hardly matter, because there is so much space. Feel yourself being that big and spacious, letting the thoughts that come into your mind be like little clouds, just drifting on by. Don't try to grab the cloud thoughts, or make them come or go. Just notice them. You might even name them — 'There's a thought about dinner. There's a worry about homework. There's a thought about when this is going to be over. And now a thought about what my friend said today.' Relax and enjoy the peace and stillness of just being the sky." After a few moments, invite them to allow their eyes to open, completing the exercise.

STROLL WITH PRESENCE

When children are small, nearly everything they do is mindful. Remember the walks you used to take with your toddler? Getting two or three houses down the street could take forever. Our little ones find everything interesting, from the sound of a bird rustling beneath a bush to those mysterious cracks in the sidewalk.

Invite your older kids to step into a greater level of awareness as you go for a walk around the neighborhood. Walk silently, and listen to the sounds around you for a minute or two. Have them notice how the air feels against their body. Is the sun warming their skin? Is there a light breeze? Encourage them to pay attention to the light — how it filters through the trees or flashes off of a nearby car. Or pretend you've just landed on Earth from another planet and everything is new. Imagine how you might see a painted fence or how you might marvel at the colors of the flowers as you pass by.

RUB HANDS TOGETHER

A very simple way to teach children to get out of their heads and back into the present moment is to have them rub their hands together rapidly for about thirty seconds, feeling the friction and growing warmth. Then have them stop and notice the tingling and heat in their hands. It's is a quick and easy way to get back into the body.

TASTE EACH BITE OF FOOD

Taste is a powerful sense, one that can bring us quickly back to the present. Suggest this to your children: "Imagine you're from a country — or another planet — where they don't have this particular food. They have never even seen it before. Take a bite and let the food sit there, rolling around in your mouth before you begin to chew. Notice the flavor of the bite — is it sweet or salty? Notice the density — is it hard or soft? How does it smell? What happens as you chew? Does the texture change as saliva is released? Avoid deciding whether you like the food and don't try to describe it. Just taste it, staying keenly aware of the tastes and sensations."

Another version of this is to invite your child to eat an apple while paying close attention to each aspect of the experience. "Tune in to your fingers wrapped around the apple. Feel its weight, its smoothness. Take a bite and hear the sound of the crunch as your teeth break the skin. Let the juices fill your mouth, noticing the taste — sweet, tart, tangy, refreshing?"

MINDFULLY LISTEN TO MUSIC

Elisha and Stefanie Goldstein, clinical psychologists and cofounders of the Center for Mindful Living, are doing wonderful work with their CALM program for teens. Their music meditation is a way for teens to have an in-body experience facilitated by something they love — music! They begin by doing a mindful check-in (having them connect to their breath, body, thoughts, and emotions) and then, as they press Play, they prompt the kids to pay attention to their full-body experience as they practice mindful listening to popular music. This activity is always a crowd pleaser!

WALK IN SLOW MOTION

A lovely mindfulness practice is to walk in slow motion, with all your awareness fixed on the tiny movements that make up each step. Drop your gaze so that you can stay internally focused. Move at a pace slower than normal, noticing how it feels as first your heel, then the ball of the foot, then your toes make contact with the ground. Pay attention to what the other foot is doing — when it lifts up, when your weight shifts. What muscles are involved in your ankles, calves, knees, and thighs? Which muscles are relaxed or tense as you move? Feel whether your steps are light or heavy. Notice how it feels to shift your balance.

You can do this activity for two or three minutes, but it gets interesting when you do mindful walking for twenty minutes or so. When I have done it at retreats, the instruction is generally for participants to avoid talking or making eye contact, staying fully present to the experience of taking each and every step.

ASK QUESTIONS TO BUILD AWARENESS

This activity comes from *The Mindful Child* by Susan Kaiser Greenland, who suggests asking questions to build more self-awareness. To increase attention, ask, "Are you focused, distracted, or in between?" To ask about wakefulness you would ask, "Do you feel sluggish, energetic, or in between?" and for physical ease you'd ask, "Is it easy to sit still, hard to sit still, or in between?" Susan says you can encourage children to answer with thumbs-up, thumbs-sideways, or thumbs-down hand signals. This is a great exercise for helping children become more aware of what they are experiencing and to communicate it both verbally and nonverbally.

FOCUS ON JUST ONE THING

Many kids believe that they can do several things at once: homework, listening to music, and maintaining a running text message conversation all at the same time. But in fact, multitasking is just rapid task-*switching*. Studies suggest that the quality of our work diminishes significantly when we split our attention between various activities. When students multitask while doing schoolwork, they understand less, have poorer recall, and find it more difficult to apply what they've studied.

If you have fallen into the habit of multitasking, try hitting reverse and letting your kids watch you giving your undivided attention to one thing at a time.

And if you find your youngster doing several things at once, suggest that he stop, take a few breaths, and collect himself from the scattered places where he's split his attention. Invite him to focus on *just one thing* for a minute or two. "Tune in to your breath or the sensations in your body, to the exclusion of anything else. Now think about whether the paragraph you just wrote for your essay really says what you wanted it to say." You might also suggest that your youngster disengage altogether and take a nature break. Breathing in the great outdoors is a great way to reorient to the present moment.

UNCURL YOUR EARS

Children have a lot of fun with this exercise. Place your thumb inside the flap at the top of each of your child's ears. With your forefinger on the outside, literally "uncurl" each ear, applying a bit of pressure as you progress down the curve to the earlobe, repeating a few times. It's a nice way to wake up the brain. Sometimes I suggest that kids do this in the morning when they're feeling groggy or before taking a test in school.

You can practice mindfulness at any time, and in fact, I have included a number of practices that can be done while in motion. But many families find it valuable to do a short practice at the same time each day. For some, a few minutes before heading off to school creates a great frame of mind for the day ahead. A quick three-minute practice can also reduce the tension of chaotic mornings. Some parents make it a habit to do a practice before bedtime, easing a child into a more relaxed state. Or you may all head to your special place to sit together just before dinner.

Don't force mindfulness on your children, like practicing piano or doing homework. Invite them to participate. If they aren't interested, let it go. Many parents give advice to their children that they have absolutely no interest in hearing. Sound familiar? When I am coaching a parent who tells me how hard he has tried to convince his child that something is good or bad for her, I ask him, "Did your daughter sign up for your class?" After a moment's pause, they laugh. We all know that kids are highly resistant to receiving input or helpful advice that they haven't asked for. So please be respectful of your children, and don't force mindfulness practices on them. Chances are, if you make these activities enjoyable, it will be a nonissue. If not, this will be a good time for you to practice nonattachment to outcomes!

Practices for Handling Big Emotions

GIVE HUGS

Oh gosh, it is probably obvious that children like hugs, but let me say a few words about them, in case affection was a taboo in your family of origin and you have underestimated its value.

Nearly all children are emotionally nourished by being held close. Physical contact with a loving caregiver regulates their still-developing, often-unstable nervous systems, settling them down. But more important, it communicates directly what a child most needs to know: that she is dearly and deeply treasured. In the wordless exchange of a long and loving embrace, everything that needs to be said is said.

It is true that some children are uncomfortable with close contact, but you will know if you have one of those kinds of youngsters. For the most part, I suggest being generous with hugs, and their close cousin, kisses on the top of the head. Some families institute a hugging policy that they call upon when things are rapidly deteriorating. They stop yelling, drop all negotiations, and open their arms wide.

Here is a description of grandparent hugs from Bunmi Laditan's "Honest Toddler." Perhaps too sugary, but I found it cute: "Grandparent hugs are mystical. If a grandparent hug were a food, it would be a marshmallow coated in chocolate sauce rolled in cotton candy gently warmed by unicorn breath." She offers steps, including: "Clear your head of any to-dos. You have nowhere to be." and "Smile like it's Christmas."

Hug your kids. If they won't let you, hug them with your eyes. They'll get the message.

LET THE TEARS FALL

Parents invest an inordinate amount of effort trying to keep their children from crying. "Don't be sad." "Dry those eyes." "It's not that bad!" As with all the miraculous systems of our body, the mechanism of crying is enormously important. Remember *dry-eyed syndrome?* This is the term used by psychologists for those children who don't care what we threaten to do or take away. Their hearts have hardened, and they are emotionally frozen.

When we begin taking time to slow down and be quietly present, painful emotions that have been long repressed may rise to the surface. Many of us remain in constant motion so we won't feel the pain of unresolved sorrow or grief, when in fact, feeling those feelings is what lets them move through and out. How wonderful to help our children learn that they can allow their emotions to be felt, including the difficult ones.

In her essay "What Makes You Cry," Annie Lalla writes,

> Feelings are internal and can often be hidden, but tears are external and thus seen by others. They are explicit visual cues that indicate: this individual needs help. A bleeding cut on your body says "pay attention, do something to heal the wound." Similarly, tears say the tribe is bleeding through the tender heart of one member. "Pay attention, go and help." Tears...your tears, are the way your body shows you what's important to you. Holding them back is a form of self-deception and a withhold [*sic*] of your deepest truth....Every uncried tear is a lost epiphany, a missed lesson, a moment that failed at aliveness....Tears lead us home.

Sometimes the most generous thing we can do for our child — or ourselves — is to sit quietly and let the tears fall. Author Marc Gafni says that our tears show us what we care about. I love that.

Encourage your children to let liquid joy and sorrow leak out of their eyes when powerful feelings show up. Honor the big emotions that move your kids, as well as yourself. Let tears lead you home, to your heart.

STAND ON ONE LEG

Kim Eng, teacher of Presence through Movement workshops, a spiritual practice that incorporates physical movement as a way of accessing the state of presence, offered this idea for stepping out of anger. The next time you find yourself in a heated argument or power struggle with your child, try standing on one leg while you argue. (The more heated the argument, the higher you lift the leg.) It's nearly impossible to continue being angry. You can have your child do the same thing. When you are standing on one leg, which seems like an absurd exercise, you will see that it isn't the exercise that is absurd, it's your ego that is being absurd. The one-legged exercise reminds you that your ego is reacting to a situation and that you can let go. Any unusual posture or movement can be used as a way to withdraw attention from the conditioned mind, becoming aware of the ego, and generating greater self-awareness.

CREATE A PEACE CORNER

Many children tell me that when they get upset by a sibling's annoying behavior or a parent's nagging, they just want to be left alone for a while. This is actually a healthy expression of self-care. One way to facilitate "alone time" is to establish a corner in your house where kids can go to recover from an emotional storm. (This is the opposite of a time-out chair or being sent to the corner because your child misbehaved.) Furnish it with a beanbag chair and a cozy blanket and call it the Peace Corner or Our Safe Spot. Place things in the space like fidget balls, pipe cleaners, Wikki Stix, a soft stuffed animal, tactile puffer balls, something pleasantly fragrant, magnets, a favorite book or toy, a Tangle stress-relief tube, or puppets. When your child is feeling out of sorts, let him know that this can be a special place where he can go to unwind and be away from everyone who may have been annoying him. You may end up using it yourself from time to time!

ESTABLISH SIGNALS

Although many parents believe that children generate meltdowns as a manipulation to get what they want, most children suffer greatly when they tip over the emotional edge and fall apart, almost always remorseful after the fact. Kids just don't always know how to keep themselves together when they're overwhelmed by big emotions.

In my work, I talk a great deal about the importance of *avoiding* parent-child problems by addressing their cause. But sometimes even our best efforts to steer clear of a child's emotional storm don't work. It can be helpful to agree on a signal your child can use to alert you when she is flooded by out-of-control feelings and needs your help. The idea is to help a child think about what she needs to come back to center, taking responsibility for preventing future meltdowns without feeling judged by us for losing her cool.

"Sweetheart, do you remember how upset you got this morning when you couldn't find the shoes you wanted to wear? It looked like you were feeling horrible — like a hurricane had started swirling inside you." Assuming she agrees, you might continue with something along these lines: "I'd like to help you when you're starting to get so upset. Can you think of what I might have said or done that would have made it easier to stop getting mad? Would you have liked it if I'd given you a hug or walked outside with you for a minute? Or maybe it would have been better if I'd just left you alone for a little bit? What do you think about coming up with a signal you could use that would tell me that you're starting to lose it? That way, I could do something helpful — like give you a hug — instead of adding to the problem by doing things like talking too much or giving advice?"

Some children will come up with a special phrase ("Sweet potatoes!"). Others might invent a hand signal (wiggling all the fingers on one hand, or pulling on an earlobe.) Or the signal could be a sound — "Whoosh!"

Realize that this is much easier to talk about when things are going well than it is to enact when a child is headed toward a tantrum. But creating a signal to nip explosive behaviors in the bud can help a child develop greater emotional awareness and mastery.

Practices for Deep Relaxing

PUT OUT FIRES

This practice can be beneficial for children who are agitated, angry, or out of sorts, since it helps carry them out of the maelstrom of upsetting thoughts. Have your child either sit or lie down, and say, "Close your eyes, and imagine you're in a tiny plane flying over every part of your body, looking for tension the way a fire-fighting plane might look for hot spots in a forest fire. It might be that your stomach feels tight, or there's a pressure in your chest. Or your hands might feel sweaty or your neck tense. Notice these sensations, and let go as you imagine flooding the area with the "water of relaxation" to put out fires of tightness and tension. As you mentally spray those areas where you are holding stress, pay attention to the wonderful feeling of relaxation that comes, and enjoy that feeling."

HAVE A BODY PART CONTEST

As goofy as it sounds, this technique has proved to be a fun way to step out of a busy mind and deepen relaxation. I lie down and close my eyes, and instead of scanning my body for tension, I search for the most relaxed body part. I actually announce to my body that we're having a contest and that the most relaxed part wins! Funny enough, as I move from head, neck, back, arms, legs and so on, I notice each part relaxing just a wee bit more so that it might "win." The sheer silliness of this activity may just appeal to your kids!

BREATHE THROUGH A STRAW

To do this exercise, you will each need a drinking straw. Invite your child to take a few normal breaths, and then have her take a breath in and slowly exhale with her lips around the straw with one hand placed about an inch from the end of the straw. The goal is to exhale so slowly that she cannot feel even a puff of air with the hand on the outer end of the straw. After two or three easy breaths, have her take another breath in, and then put the straw back to her lips and exhale slowly so that again, her hand does not feel any wind. Eventually this exercise can be done without a straw, by simply placing a hand outside the nose or mouth as you exhale, trying again to let the air out so gently that there is no felt puff of air.

GIVE YOUR CHILD A CALMING BRACELET

Ceremoniously put a little bracelet on your child's wrist, calling it "your special calming bracelet." Then sit together doing one of the quieting activities that has proved successful in helping your child feel peaceful and calm. When you complete the exercise, have him touch the bracelet, suggesting that he pour his peaceful feelings into the bracelet to saturate it with calmness. "When you feel restless or stirred up, touch your bracelet and remember this wonderful feeling of calm."

LONG SWING

I learned this exercise while doing vision training but have found that it not only helps my eyes relax by breaking up the stare from being on the computer, but it also helps me restore a feeling of relaxation. It may have something to do with the steady motion, like being rocked in our mother's bellies.

Have your child stand with feet about shoulder width apart and say, "With your eyes open, twist the upper part of your body to the right and then to the left, keeping your feet on the floor but allowing each heel to lift up as you twist to the opposite side. Let your eyes land wherever they will, rather than fixating on any one spot. In fact, don't *try* to see anything. Let your eyes rapidly alight on hundreds of spots without fixating on any one place in particular, while you swing from one side to the other." Although the benefits increase the longer you do this exercise, even three or four minutes can be very calming.

DO CHILD'S POSE

Yoga offers a wide variety of postures that promote relaxation. One of my favorites for children — appropriately named — is Child's Pose. Start in a kneeling position and drop your bottom to your heels while stretching your body down and forward onto the mat. Lay your arms alongside your body on the floor, your stomach on top of your thighs, and allow your forehead to rest on the mat. This posture relaxes the entire body and is one of many poses helpful in alleviating stress.

Practices for the Whole Family

SHARE APPRECIATIONS

When I have a family counseling session, I often begin with a round of appreciations. Each member takes turns standing up and telling each person in turn one specific thing they appreciate about them based on the past week. "Daddy, I appreciated that you went bike riding with me. (Older brother) Max, I appreciate that you let me play with you in your room instead of kicking me out. (Little sister) Cassie, I appreciate that you helped me find my shoes. I forgot I'd taken them off in the backyard, but you remembered. Mommy, I appreciate that you put almonds in my cereal the way I like them." As each person waits to hear what the speaker is about to say about them, their faces have an expectant, almost beatific glow. I never fail to be touched by these simple expressions, and the way hearts soften. Many families institute this practice regularly. Being appreciated by someone almost instantly changes how we feel about him, even if he is your annoying big brother!

INJECT MORE FUN

The Fun Factor seems to be seriously missing in many children's lives. Below are a few ideas for injecting more playfulness into your daily routine. I highly recommend making it a practice to play more with your children!

- Chase your kids around the house.
- Blow bubbles.
- Roughhouse with them regularly.
- March around the table before everyone leaves the dinner table, accompanied by tambourines and kazoos.
- Play hide-and-seek.
- Have a pillow fight.
- Have each member of the family bring a joke to share at the dinner table.
- Sing a song of thanks before you eat.
- Plan a karaoke night with your neighbors.
- Have a family disco party, or learn square dancing together.
- Cook together. Be your child's sous chef, letting him plan the menu as you do the chopping and slicing.
- Play marbles (still one of my favorite games).
- Have a riddle contest.
- Stage a neighborhood talent show, with your family joining forces for an act.
- Speak in a foreign accent when you ask your kids to clean up their toys. Whisper. Command them as though you're the Queen of Lala-land.
- Schedule a monthly date night with each of your kids. Go somewhere you've never been.
- Have breakfast for dinner. Eat out on the grass, or have an old-fashioned picnic at the park, replete with egg tosses and relay races with friends.

- Swing on the swings together.
- Play horseshoes, beanbag toss, darts.
- Do calligraphy (a very mindful yet creative activity).
- Splash in a wading pool.
- Draw on the sidewalk together with chalk. Make a family masterpiece!
- Have a staring contest — no one blinks! Or a smiling contest, with each of you trying your best not to smile.
- Stage a family drum circle. Bongos, pots and pans with wooden spoons — anything will do. If you have a dancer in the family, he or she can move to the beat.
- Play hooky with your kids once a year: drive *toward* school, then drive on by and head out on an unplanned adventure for the day. "Shall we turn right or left?" Make it up as you go.

Ralph Waldo Emerson said, "It is a happy talent to know how to play." Having fun with your children is one of the quickest ways to change the pH of the relationship (chapter 3) and restore connection. Enjoy!

THREE PLEASURES A DAY

This is a fun activity to do with your children. It will help shift the focus from mental activities (often involving something with a plug, screen, or battery) to the pleasures that come from simply inhabiting a human body. It is adapted from Martha Beck's *The Joy Diet*.

Invite each person in the family to complete the following sentences aloud by listing five things that they enjoy in each category. One of you can take notes. Then, enjoy at least three of these pleasures a day!

1. I love the taste of:
2. I love the sight of:
3. I love the feel of:
4. I love the smell of:
5. I love the sound of:

What you discover may steer you all toward wonderful activities that have long been ignored. Remembering that you love the smell of lilacs might remind you of how much you enjoy visiting a florist — an easy way to uplift your spirits. Or you may recall how relaxing it is to listen to the sound of the birds, sending you more often to a park bench to drink in their song.

MINDFUL DRAWING

Drawing with a child is a great way to settle into the present moment together. Have your youngster choose a simple object and share the instruction to simply draw what you see. Allow the left, language-based, analytical side of your brain to quiet down as you simply draw what is in front of you. Notice details. Walk around the object to see it from different angles. This is a great activity to do with children to awaken awareness to the "what is" in front of us.

STORYTELLING

In this era of digital overload, many children are losing the ability to form pictures in their mind, contributing to a decrease in their willingness to enjoy the pleasures of a good book. Storytelling entertains, activates the imagination, and calms children down. There are a variety of ways to engage children in the timeless art of telling stories. Cuddle up, invent an unusual character, and see what happens as you start weaving a tale. Don't worry about whether you're "good" at storytelling. Your kids will be entertained by your effort.

Another option is to create "take-turn" stories. Offer an opening sentence and then have each of your children add a line or two as you go around in a circle, developing the narrative. Their participation ensures that they will stay alert and engaged. You may also choose to listen to stories. There are gifted actors who deliver dramatic audio performances for children. One of my favorites is Jim Weiss, from Great Hall Productions.

Telling (and listening to) stories is relaxing, builds connection, and develops children's ability to stay focused. Have fun with it!

JUST LISTEN

It goes without saying, but I'll say it anyway. One of the best ways to connect with your child is to drop what you're doing and listen to her. Be interested in what she is interested in. Ask questions. Talk about spiders or Elmo or climate change. When we make ourselves fully available to our children to learn more about their interior life with openness and curiosity, we restore connection and strengthen attachment.

In chapter 6, I referred to an exercise I call the Three Yeses that facilitates greater mutual understanding and empathy. Here is an example of this exercise from a session I had with a mother and her son. It begins with Thomas speaking for a few minutes to his mom about something that's been bothering him. Mom has agreed to listen carefully without interrupting, rolling her eyes, or defending herself. At the end, she is instructed to get three yeses from Thomas so that he feels heard and validated, and then they switch.

THOMAS: "Mom, it makes me really mad when you are so cranky in the morning. I don't like it when you come into my room all mad and yelling at me. You're a lot nicer to Jen. It's not fair. I'm tired in the morning and I wish you would let me sleep more. I don't see why I have to get up at 6:45. We don't even leave till 7:30, and I don't need as much time to get ready as she does. I don't even want to eat breakfast but you make me and I'm not even hungry. I could just have a breakfast bar in the car. But you still make me get up and sit at the table, and I wish you'd let me stay in bed longer. I'm really tired. That's all I wanna say."

MOM: "Thanks, Thomas. So, one thing I heard you say is that you don't see why you have to get up so early. It seems like you can get ready in less than forty-five minutes."

THOMAS: "Yes." (I hold up one finger, indicating that mom has gotten one yes.)

MOM: "I also heard you say that you really don't like it when I yell in the morning. That really doesn't feel good."

THOMAS: "Yep. That's right." (I hold up two fingers.)

MOM: "And I think I heard you say that you wish you could have your breakfast in the car."

THOMAS: "No, I just want to eat a bar in the car. Not a whole breakfast."

MOM: "Okay. You wish you could have a breakfast bar in the car. So you could stay in bed longer."

THOMAS: "Yes!" (I hold up three fingers, confirming that mom got her three yeses.)

MOM: "Okay — got it. Thank you for sharing all that with me."

Now it's mom's turn. She gets to respond — respectfully — to what Thomas has said, and it is now his turn to get three yeses so she also feels heard.

MOM: "I understand that you're really tired in the morning, and it's super hard to get out of bed. But it's hard for me, too. Every morning when I head down the hall to your room, I get tense because I don't feel up to facing another battle with you. I have to be at work by 8:30, and if I don't drop you guys off at school right on time, I'll be late, and then I'll have to deal with my boss giving me dirty looks all day — maybe even thinking I don't take my job seriously enough. I wish we could start our mornings off in a friendlier way because I love you and it hurts my heart to fight with you. It hurts both of us. I wish you would go to bed on time so you weren't so tired, so we could start our day out in a loving way without my feeling so stressed from the very start."

THOMAS: "Okay. Um, one thing I guess you said was that if we're late for school you get in trouble at work if you're late."

MOM: "Yes, that's about right. I don't get in trouble — like being sent to a principal's office or anything — but my boss notices and doesn't like it at all." (I hold up one finger.)

THOMAS: "Okay. And then I heard you say that you get tensed up when you're coming into my room because you don't want to have another fight."

MOM: "Yes." (I hold up two fingers.)

THOMAS: "Hmm...I can't remember what else."

I invite mom to speak for another minute or so, and then we turn it back to Thomas.

THOMAS: "Oh, yeah. You also said that you wish that we could start our day out happier. You said you love me and you don't like it when we don't have a good morning."

MOM: "That is very true. Thank you for listening, Thomas. I really appreciate it." (I hold up the third finger, showing Thomas that he has gotten three yeses.)

THOMAS: (very shyly) "Okay."

What I have repeatedly found from doing this exercise is that the simple act of feeling heard and validated opens people up to experiencing more empathy for the person they were angry with. This helps create a climate in which new possibilities or agreements can be forged. Another way of saying this is that each person shifts from feeling like the other's enemy to being on the same team. It is an easy but powerful exercise.

WEAVE IN A MORNING GOOD-BYE RITUAL

Weaving in a quick mindfulness practice before sending a child off to school only takes a minute and can set him up to have a much better day. Adding an element that fosters connection can also make partings easier for children who have a difficult time with separation. It might be something like taking three deep breaths together while holding hands. It could be a three-second hug, or a little song that the two of you make up. Children love rituals. The more you make anchoring yourselves to feelings of gratitude or connection a part of your child's daily routine, the more likely it will become something she continues to do on her own.

DELIVER A SMILE

One of the simplest ways we humans connect with one another is by sharing a smile. It is a universal way of touching another's heart, building trust, and fostering empathy. On top of that, there are actually health benefits to smiling! It reduces blood pressure, relaxes the body, releases endorphins, and helps diminish stress. A smile delivered lovingly to a child as she races through breakfast or to a wife as she walks in the door can be transformative.

A sweet side note: Obstetrician Dr. Carey Andrew-Jaja sings "Happy Birthday" to every newborn he delivers. So far more than eight thousand children have been welcomed into the world by his song. Imagine how it would affect our child if every time he walked into a room, we quietly celebrated his presence. It is a gift to a child to feel so loved.

OFFER A LOVE FEAST

We all want to feel we are appreciated for who we are. When people visit my website and opt in for my newsletter, they are sent a video with an exercise called Love Flooding. In the video, I invite parents to write down at least ten things they love and appreciate about their child and then set aside time to read their list to their son or daughter. Many parents have told me that this little activity — one that takes just a few minutes — has dramatically improved their relationship with their child.

When we let a child know that she is cherished by us for who she is, we are offering her a feast of our love. I highly recommend telling those you love the things about them that delight you.

Practices for Manifesting a Happy and Fulfilling Life

SET INTENTIONS

Most days, before I walk into my office to start a session with a client, I set an intention for clarity, presence, and wisdom. Each year I host a *Parenting with Presence* summit, a series of dialogues held over four days with a variety of notable people such as Dr. Jane Goodall, Arianna Huffington, Jon Kabat-Zinn, Alanis Morissette, and Congressman Tim Ryan. Before beginning, I take a moment with each guest to set an intention that our discussion may unfold in a way that allows us to reach the minds and hearts of parents in every part of the world, uplifting, inspiring, and supporting. When I get in my car, I close my eyes to set an intention for safe passage before driving off.

Teaching children to set intentions is easy. Simply help them describe, in positive terms, how they would like something to go

— perhaps enjoying a school performance or feeling confident during an upcoming test. Stepping into a situation with a clear intention can make a huge difference in our experience of it.

SHOW GRATITUDE

Gratitude is at the cornerstone of everything I have talked about in this book. It changes everything — our relationship to whatever is going on in our life, our ability to accept the people we interact with, and our capacity to enjoy the moment we're in. Appreciation transforms the most challenging experience into one that we can embrace. I could write a book on gratitude — and many have! Here are some ideas that you may want to incorporate into your life.

When you feel appreciation for something someone has done, let him know. It's easy to forget to acknowledge the kindnesses we are shown by others, but it is also easy to let them know we noticed and are grateful. A quick "thank you" in person is fine, especially when you pause to actually feel grateful while you are speaking. A text message or email can let someone know you recognized their effort. A quick phone call is lovely. But there's nothing like handwriting a note, addressing and stamping it, and sending it off in the mail, knowing the recipient will have the pleasure of reading and rereading your words of gratitude. Letter writing is a lost art — and one I think we should revive. If you're so inclined, you may even encourage your kids to write notes of thanks — but only if it is done in a relaxed atmosphere. Forcing kids to write thank-you notes can discourage a child from doing them for the rest of their lives!

PUT A DIME IN THE BLAME JAR

I wrote earlier about the importance of taking responsibility for our mistakes. While others may provide us with *opportunities* for

justifying our unkind behavior, we need to help children learn
that they are responsible for their actions. Blaming keeps us from
being accountable and making the changes that would bring us
closer to happiness, regardless of whether people or circumstances conform to our liking. A blame jar can help everyone in
the family shift out of victim mode. The idea is simple: if someone
points the finger at someone else for making a mistake, she puts
a dime in the jar. (Some parents include whining or complaining
as behaviors that cost a dime!) This activity can be an important
element in raising the awareness that we are the architects of our
lives rather than at the mercy of things we cannot control.

TAKE A SIX-MINUTE DRIVE

Think about a place that is a short drive from home, and try adding this activity as a ritual you institute every time you drive to
that place. From the time you leave the house until you arrive at
the grocery store, school, or park, declare aloud the things you
are grateful for. It's that easy. "I'm so glad I have this warm
jacket on such a cold morning." "I am thankful for that yummy
smoothie we just had." "I'm grateful for you guys — you little
munchkins!" By the end of the ride, you may be surprised by how
great you all feel — and grateful!

DO A THIRTY-SECOND APPRECIATION

Here is something you can pause and do right now. Look around
and let your eyes land on something in your immediate environment. Choose something ordinary, something you've seen countless times before. Perhaps it is the glass of water beside you. Look
at it carefully. Pause to appreciate it. Consider the person who
designed the glass, how she thought about what it would feel like
to hold it, and to drink from it — how she considered the size of

your hand as she determined its dimensions and the way your lip would feel as you placed it to your mouth. Think about the water — the person who helped configure the filtering plant to remove contaminants so that you could safely quench your thirst. Allow yourself to relax into an appreciation for this simple glass of water and all that has gone into manifesting it on the table beside you. You can do this throughout your day, with virtually unlimited objects. Sense the experience of gratitude settling into you.

Another thirty-second exercise is to touch your hand to your heart as you review your blessings, reconnecting to your heart and spirit. Let gratitude spread through your chest like a warm glow, opening you up to the miracle of the moment. Making this a daily practice can transform your life. You may even want to set an alarm on your smartphone to remind you to do this every hour or two to solidify an attitude of gratitude!

MAKE PAPER CHAINS OF GRATITUDE

This is another easy activity you can do with your children. Cut out at least twenty strips of paper and on each strip write down something you're grateful for. You can then make a paper chain that you hang in the kitchen or living room — or outside your front door — as a reminder of gratitude. So fun!

PREVIEW THE DAY

Before your eyes even open in the morning, preview the day to come and relax into a place of gratitude for each of the people you are likely to encounter — children, spouse, neighbor, boss, coworkers. Generate at least five things about each person that you appreciate. This can definitely make your day go easier and is also a great practice to do with children before they head off to school.

VELCRO THE GOOD

Neuropsychologist Rick Hanson has coined the term *Velcro-Teflon syndrome*. He says that because Mother Nature is more concerned with our survival than our enjoyment of any particular event, we are wired to remember negative experiences much more intensely than positive ones. The threat of a wild boar makes more impact than a little bird tweeting its song!

So negative experiences stick to us like Velcro, lodging themselves in our consciousness, where we review them again and again...and again, often as we're trying to fall asleep. ("I can't believe my boss didn't thank me for staying late to work on that project. He doesn't appreciate how hard I work! I put in so much time there.") Thankfully, we can change the pattern of spiraling into negative thinking.

The longer we hold a *positive* moment in our awareness, the more neurons will fire and wire together, creating a hospitable climate in our brain for happiness. Therefore, if we want our positive experiences to stick (rather than slide off our Teflon coating), we need to remain focused on them for at least twenty seconds. Hanson says, "The more you get your neurons firing about positive facts, the more they'll be wiring up positive neural structures."

Create a gratitude journal and write about positive experiences from your day. Make a drawing of something special that happened that you feel grateful for. Or brag to others — or out loud to yourself — about the good that comes your way. All these activities will take at least twenty seconds, ensuring that your focus makes the neuronal shift toward positivity.

NOTICE THE POSITIVE

When you experience something pleasing — the taste of a juicy blueberry, your kids laughing together, the sun warming your skin — allow yourself to soak in good feelings about it. Let positive feelings spread through your body like a wildfire, igniting a heightened alertness to joy. Know that while you are staying aware of this good experience, your neurons are firing and wiring together, creating more durable pathways for happiness.

SAY, "CANCEL, CANCEL"

We cannot choose our first thought, but we *can* choose our second one. In other words, a negative thought might drop into our mind, but that doesn't mean we have to continue down its dark and dreary road. If a negative or limiting belief lands in your head, such as, "I can't believe how selfish Jonathon is" or "I'll never be able to figure out how to put this juicer together," say, "Cancel, Cancel." The idea is that you immediately nip in the bud the potential for a downward spiral into negativity.

Practices for Parents to Do on Their Own

TOSS DOWN THE ANCHOR

One of the greatest predictors of how my day is going to go is whether or not I'm tethered to my spirit. It's analogous to a ship at sea; one that is free floating can drift off course for miles, while a ship that is anchored — even in the midst of rough waters — will remain wherever the anchor was tossed down.

Regardless of what tasks or activities await us when we open our eyes to face a new morning, most of us feel pressure to get started. There are children to awaken, breakfasts to prepare, lunches to pack, emails to check — the list is endless. Many of us operate from a sense of urgency — the sooner I can get started, the sooner I'll be done and the pressure will be off. But the truth, of course, is that the minute we check one thing off the list, another pops up in its place. We will never be done, caught up, or complete with everything we have to take care of.

We shortchange ourselves when we leap into the day without making contact with the touchstone within, even for a moment or two. And here is what I have discovered: That beautiful feeling inside is the secret sauce that makes everything better. When I focus on my spirit, I feel so much better, and so much more myself; I shake my head in wonder that I skip days or don't spend more time doing something that brings me so much joy and peace.

But I forget. It seems that life is orchestrated in such a way as to require me to *choose* that inner experience, to consciously turn away from the seduction of the outer world to swim in the waters of the inner one. It's not easy. I am drawn to what's going on outside myself. Potential distractions are everywhere: The newspaper. The television. Emails. The garden that needs watering. The phone calls that need to be returned. And this is life *without* children underfoot! For parents of little ones, carving out a few minutes to drink from the peaceful well within is a challenge, I know.

And I have also found, over the forty plus years I have meditated, that the feeling inside wants to be courted. It's like a tentative but extraordinary lover. When I set a clear intention that if only for a few moments, I am going to give all of myself to that inner experience and I keep turning toward that feeling when my mind wanders, I am rewarded with an experience that defies description. It is holy and divine, sweet and tender. I become who I am, and my heart does a little song and dance with happiness that I have taken the time to feed it what it most wants and loves and needs. From this place, I can move through my day with that feeling still humming in the background, at least some of the day, or at least until the noise of the outside world gets terribly loud. But even then, the deepest part of me remembers what is more real inside me, and I don't lose myself quite so badly in the rush and tumble.

Meditation is a practice. It's not a pill we can pop. It takes time to get to know ourselves as who we truly are. It is an investment. Not everyone wants to go deeply within, and that is fine. We should each follow the call of our hearts.

But following the call of our hearts requires us to get quiet and listen. As you tune in to what brings you a sense of peace or joy, pay attention. Court that feeling. Bring it flowers. Send it love letters. That feeling beneath your identity as a wife, husband, partner, mother, father is who you really are. Just like your child, it wants to be seen and loved. It wants your time and attention. Investing in that *you* — beyond the external identity or role you play — will pay off in spades. Make time for it. Throw down the anchor to connect with your inner self for a moment before going about the business of your day. I think you'll be glad you did.

DO NOTHING

Choose a fifteen-minute time slot and find a place where you can be alone. (I know this is easier said than done, but stay with me here.) It might be a walking trail, your back porch, or even your car. Try to ensure that for those fifteen minutes you will not be interrupted. Martha Beck describes this as putting up the No Vacancy sign in your life.

She goes on to say that the next step is either to sit in meditation or to do a mindless, repetitive activity that keeps your body busy such as walking, Rollerblading, or jogging. Watch grass blowing in a field, or witness the ripples moving across a pond.

Next she invites you to vacate your mind. "The typical human mind is like a supercomputer possessed by the soul of a demented squirrel. It's constantly calculating, anticipating, remembering, fantasizing, worrying, hoarding, bouncing frenetically from thought to thought to thought." At this stage, you simply watch your thoughts without judging them. You might picture the thoughts in your head as small, yapping dogs. You are the big elephant lumbering down the road as the harmless little dogs yip and yap.

The last step is to create a mental image of a sanctuary where you can anchor yourself in times of stress or chaos. Call to mind a special place where you feel peaceful and still, a place where the world stops and you come to a feeling of deep rest and contentment. You can visit this place in your imagination during your fifteen minutes of Doing Nothing. This practice is wonderful for helping restore a sense of peace and balance in your life.

MAKE CONTACT

Here is an activity I sometimes do when I am in an airport, although I've done it other times as well. I walk through the terminal specifically watching for anyone who is available for contact — a glance, a friendly smile, a nod. When I play this game, I usually notice that it is difficult to find someone who isn't hurrying and scurrying around, looking at his watch or fussing at his children to stay close. But now and then I hit the jackpot and get a lovely reminder from another pair of eyes that no matter where we're going, we are each just here and now, and all is well.

APPRECIATE YOURSELF

This exercise can be one of the hardest; when I do it with my clients it is sometimes like pulling teeth to get them started. But it is very powerful.

Think about the qualities in yourself that you appreciate: *kindness, generosity, patience, a sense of humor.* Include anything you like about yourself. If you are having a hard time, ask your friends to tell you five things they appreciate about you. (If that is also difficult, tell them it's a required assignment for a class you're taking!) Read your list daily, adding things as often as possible.

Until we recognize our own beauty and goodness, it will be difficult for us to receive love and cooperation from others. Make sure you know what a gift you are to us all.

TUNE IN WHEN YOU ARE TRIGGERED

Sometimes we get triggered because our child's behavior is in direct conflict with our beliefs. If you grew up in a household where it was expected that children should instantly do what they're asked, or should never talk back to their parents, then you are likely to feel a real reaction coming on when your kids refuse to pitch in, or they sass back.

We may also get triggered when our child behaves in a way that is foreign to our innate temperament. A loud child is more likely to push the buttons of his mild-mannered mother. Or we might lose a grip on our composure because we believe we aren't living up to the expectations of people whose opinion means a great deal to us — our spouse, friends, mother-in-law, or favorite parenting "expert."

When you realize that you are out of alignment with your own inner parenting wisdom, try the following exercise.

STEP 1. Become quiet and still. Tune in to what is taking place — your little boy demanding pasta and butter or your daughter refusing to turn off the TV. Simply become aware of how you are feeling inside.

STEP 2. If an onslaught of thoughts starts fueling your upset, ask, "Whose voice am I hearing in my head right now?" My mother or father's? A stern teacher's?

STEP 3. Instead of trying to get rid of that voice, make friends with it, assuming that it is well intentioned. What is its purpose? What is it trying to spare you from or help you see? Perhaps it wants to warn you that you aren't being assertive enough. Or it may be suggesting that you're perilously out of control.

STEP 4. Look for the need underneath that voice. Perhaps it is saying: *I am afraid that you don't know how to handle your son. I'm worried that if I don't scare you or criticize your parenting, you will stop trying to rein in his aggressive tendencies.*

STEP 5. Jot down what you learn from this insight. Say to that voice within yourself: *I get the message, I appreciate it, and here's what I'm going to do about it.*

This activity may be done in conjunction with therapy or a parenting class in which you are in a committed process to learn more about what derails your efforts to stay calmly and lovingly in charge. It isn't easy, but it is always illuminating.

DANCE YOUR WAY OUT OF ANGER

One of the quickest ways to get anger out of your body is to dance. Put on one of your favorite toe-tappers, and get moving! By the end of a song or two, you may even have forgotten what got you so hot and bothered! I often start off my day with something lively or take dance breaks after focused writing to get back into my body and the juicy thrill of being alive.

NAME WHAT YOU MISS

Being present means making contact with life as it is, right now. It means choosing to be here, even if "here" isn't quite what you'd pictured. It means being present with the sound of your children laughing — or arguing — in the next room. It means being present as you sit on the piano bench helping your son practice as he stumbles through the notes.

But sometimes, before we can fully be present to what is in

front of us, we have to grieve for what we have lost, or at least what we think we've lost.

Take a few moments to get quiet. Place your hand on your heart as you breathe, and step into a place of real kindness toward yourself. Acknowledge the effort you make each day from the moment you awaken until you collapse into bed at night. Soften your heart to the ways you have had to stretch beyond yourself and the things you have had to let go of.

Ask this question, and wait for an answer without forcing one to come: *"What am I missing from the life I was living before I had children?"* Be still and wait quietly. If no answer comes to mind, that's fine. If you sense or hear an answer that doesn't immediately make sense, let it lead you where it will.

It is important to stay in a loving and kind place toward all of yourself, allowing anything to be true, even if it isn't the truest truth or the whole truth. Perhaps you miss preparenting dinners when you could sit down from start to finish without popping up to get something for someone. You may miss leisurely time to be romantic with your partner. You might miss long baths, or walks alone in the woods, or simply a mind that isn't constantly keeping track of where your children are, how they're doing, or what they *should* be doing. You might miss uninterrupted time to write, read, or meditate. Or you might just miss who you were before you became so inextricably entwined with others — perhaps you were more lighthearted and relaxed or more focused and seemingly productive.

Reflect on this question. You may want to talk aloud or journal about what comes up. Again, if nothing shows up, that's fine. Don't force yourself to miss something you don't miss. But give yourself space for flushing out the hidden things that may impair your ability to show up completely for your life.

ASK YOURSELF SOME DIFFICULT QUESTIONS

Many times we have trouble being attuned with and present to our child because, as discussed in chapter 3, our vision of raising children doesn't quite match up to reality. It may even be radically different from what we expected, leaving us disappointed, discouraged, or even regretful.

None of this means we don't love our children or that we wish we didn't have them. It just means that we have feelings we need to face rather than sweeping them under the rug. It is our expectations that get us into trouble. If you were sure that having a baby would solidify a marriage that was on the rocks, you may have discovered that parenting adds to marital stress rather than eliminating it. If you imagined that having a baby would win you the approval of your parents, you may find that it also exposes you to their ongoing criticism about how you're parenting. And if you believed that having a baby would fill an emptiness in your heart and soul, you have probably found out that it does not, and cannot, without enormous cost to your child.

That said, children do add to our lives immeasurably. They sometimes even strengthen marriages, create stronger bonds with extended family, and fill our hearts with a love we could not have imagined. The problem is that children don't *always* do those things for us. And most important, it is not their *job* to improve our marriages and family relations or vanquish our loneliness. Just like that line in *Jerry Maguire* that precipitated ridicule — "You complete me" — it is not our children's job to complete us. When we raise our kids with that kind of neediness, we disturb the natural hierarchy of dependency. Our kids are meant to lean on us — not be the answer to our unresolved needs.

Below are a few questions you may find useful as you reflect on the expectations you brought to your parenting life. I urge you to be honest but also very gentle with yourself. We all have expectations about raising children. We all hope that adding kids will make our lives better. We all have wounds from our childhoods that we hope to heal as we grow older. If you discover that you believed your kids would win you approval, get you more attention, or make you feel less alone, that's okay. If some very painful realizations come up, please seek the support of a trusted professional to help move through those old feelings.

I once heard an interview with a mother who was stalking her twenty-seven-year-old daughter — showing up at her work, hanging around her favorite coffee shop, and calling her throughout the day to "check in." Her daughter was mortified and desperate to have some space.

When the mother was challenged by the interviewer, she declared with great emotion, "I love my daughter! I have been a mother my whole life! It's what I do! It's who I am!" The psychologist urged her to pursue interests she had before she'd had children. She replied, "I don't have any other interests. I've never done anything else. I am a mother." She had so identified with the role of parent that she had lost a sense of herself as a separate person. And in the process, she was clipping her daughter's wings.

Here are some questions to reflect on:

What did you hope parenting would do for you? What changes did you imagine it would bring about in your life?

Was there an empty feeling that you hoped would be filled by having a child?

How has real-life parenting failed to match up to your expectations?

Are there times that you wish you could freeze-frame? Do you miss earlier stages of your child's life in ways that make it difficult to accept who they are now?

Again, take your time, and go easy with this exercise. It's all okay.

UNRAVEL YOUR FEAR OF BEING JUDGED

Many parents feel especially triggered by their child's misbehavior when they are out in public or with extended family. They may suffer from what psychologist Mary Pipher calls *imaginary audience syndrome*, a term she coined to describe adolescent girls' heightened self-consciousness. But parents can also suffer from this affliction, believing that other people are scrutinizing their every move, judging them ruthlessly every time they fail to subdue a child's tantrums, or their child forgets her manners.

When we are suffering from imaginary audience syndrome we are terrified of losing status with those we think we need to impress, moving into Lawyer or Dictator mode to try to control our child's behavior so we can look good to those around us.

The following questions can help you get to the root of these feelings of shame or heightened self-consciousness.

1. Whose judgment do you most fear?
2. What concerns you about having this person thinking poorly about your parenting?
3. What would having this person's approval give you?
4. What else would you gain from this person's approval?
5. And what else?
6. Is there any way you could get the things you wrote in answer to 3 to 5 without securing that person's approval?

This exercise can uncover some difficult truths but can also be invaluable in liberating us to live with greater authenticity, imperfections and all.

SEE YOUR CHILD WITHOUT A NAME

Sometimes we trip over personality and ego, losing sight of who we and our children are beneath names, labels, and long-held perceptions. Try this: Forget your child's name for a moment. Forget what she's good at or the headaches she gives you over homework or chores. Forget that you are her mother or father. Simply step back and regard your child as a spirit poured into the container that is her body, here to journey alongside you in this most intimate way. You may find it easier to do this exercise when your child is sleeping, but it can be lovely to spend a few minutes in the wakeful company of your child, trying to see him or her as a beloved brother or sister of your soul. Just don't forget that, in *this* lifetime, at this time, you are playing the role of parent; while you and your children are equals on a soul level, down here on Earth, you're still the grown-up in charge.

SAY, "THERE, THERE"

Parents are often masters at offering comfort to their children. We fuss over boo-boos, cluck over owies, and pour mommy or daddy love into broken hearts.

How sad then, that we are sometimes so cruel to ourselves when we are hurting. "I should have known better!" "I shouldn't let that bother me!"

I have repeatedly said that parenting is hard. It is. It's impossible, really. And therefore it is impossible not to have really tough days. That is one of the reasons I love the following practice and urge you to make it your own.

When you are feeling overwhelmed, or you've come apart at the seams, touch your heart in the same loving way you would your hurting little boy or girl, and say, "There, there." I want you to say it *out loud*. Parents are no less deserving of loving-kindness and comfort than their children, and yet we are exceptionally stingy about acknowledging how tough it sometimes is to keep it all together.

The next time you feel stuck or confused, or you fall into a state of remorse over something you did, say, "There, there." And be sure to pat your heart as you do.

TAKE BABY STEPS TOWARD CHANGE

In all my writings, courses, and presentations, I try not only to inform and inspire but also to help parents make *practical* changes in their lives. With that in mind, I'd like to invite you to think about what you have read in this book that made *particular* sense to you. What grabbed your attention or prompted you to think about your own parenting life? You may find it useful to do a quick scan through the book to see what jumps out or reminds you of something you'd like to incorporate into your life.

Pick two things you would like to work on in the next three months. Perhaps you want to commit to acknowledging nonjudgmentally whatever you are feeling when you find yourself getting upset. You may decide you want to be kinder to yourself — more ruthless about challenging the negative things you say to yourself. Maybe you want to slow down and be more present with your kids. Or you may decide you'd like to commit to apologizing more readily, taking ownership for mistakes.

Set realistic goals for making the changes you have chosen. If you decide to change the tone of voice you use with your kids *and* how much time you spend with them *and* how often you're on your digital devices *and* how present you stay with your feelings when you get upset, *and* how calmly you handle stress...well, you get the picture. It's no good trying to change everything at once. At any rate, I have no doubt that much of how you are parenting is already terrific! I just want you to focus on two things that would make a substantive difference in your daily life. Or even one!

In your journal, please describe two changes that you would like to work on in the next three months. Below each intention, write a sentence or two about *why* you want to institute this shift.

How will your life improve as a result? Here's what it will look like (This exercise can also be found on my website, www.Susan Stiffelman.com/PWPextras):

Two changes I'd like to make in the next three months:

1. Why I want to work on this (How will my life be better?):
2. Evidence of change (How will I know that these changes are underway?):

You will lose your way. Just as you are instructed to gently bring your focus back to your breath if your mind wanders during mindfulness practices, be kind to yourself if you drift from your intended new behavior. You may find yourself nagging when you promised you wouldn't or getting lost online when you committed to hitting the Off switch after a certain amount of time. Be patient. Be kind to yourself.

At the end of each day, jot down any progress you made toward making these two changes, even if you have to get out your magnifying glass to find something! Change happens baby step by baby step. There will be days when you seem to move backward, slipping and stumbling along. That's to be expected. Just commit to making an effort, and write or record at least two or three bits of evidence that suggest you're moving forward with your intentions.

A story is told about a shepherd boy who wanted to be strong enough to lift a sheep but found it impossible, lamenting to his father that he was too weak. His father picked out a newborn lamb and gave his son the instruction to carry the lamb around its enclosure every day, without fail. The boy thought his father's directions were useless. After all, the baby lamb was so light and so tiny; he wanted to be able to carry a full-grown sheep! But he obliged his father, carrying the baby lamb around its enclosure each day, not noticing that every day, the lamb was growing bigger — and the boy's muscles were growing stronger. Finally, as months went by, the boy realized that he had become capable of carrying what was now a full-grown sheep.

If you commit to living with greater awareness, acknowledging any and all small successes each day, then change in your family will be inevitable. You will be able to carry the sheep. Just start — today — by lifting the little lamb.

WEAR A RUBBER BAND

This exercise is an easy way to make practical and lasting changes. I have used it not only with adults but also with children, with great success.

Choose one thing you would like to stop doing. It could be yelling at your kids. It might be blaming others. Place a rubber band on your wrist as you announce your desire to stop doing that thing. I sometimes have each member of a family pick a behavior they would like to work on and then invite them to all ceremoniously put their rubber band on while declaring their intention. "I hereby place this rubber bands on my wrist with the intention of using a nicer tone of voice with everybody!" "I hereby place this rubber band on my wrist with the intention of not teasing my little sister!"

If you slip up and do the behavior you're trying to stop, move the rubber band to the other wrist. The goal? Keep the rubber band on the same wrist for twenty-one consecutive days.

The idea is that it takes about twenty-one days to change a habit. So if you have a physical reminder with you wherever you go, it becomes easier to stay aware of your intention to change a behavior.

Epilogue

In India a story is told of a man who leaves his village to make his fortune. Some years later, as he journeys back home with his riches, a thief claiming to be a fellow traveler joins him. As they travel together each day, the wealthy man talks about the money he made and all the things he is going to do now that he is rich. Every night the two of them share lodging. When the wealthy man steps out for his evening meal, his companion searches the room from top to bottom for the money the man claims he is bringing back to his village.

On their final day, as the man nears his village, the thief confesses. "I must tell you that I am a thief. It was my plan to steal your riches, but each night when you left the room, I searched high and low and never found anything. Tell me, now that you are safely delivered to your village — did you really have all that money? Where did you hide it?"

His companion replies, "I knew you were a thief from the moment we first met and that you would be trying to steal from me all that I had worked so hard to earn. That is why I hid my money where you would never find it."

"Where? Where did you hide it?"

The man replied simply, "Under your pillow."

We gain true freedom when we realize that everything we could ever want or need for is already ours. But we forget.

In *Conversations with God*, Neale Donald Walsch invites us to imagine that God delivers us into human life with amnesia. We forget who we are so that we might experience the great joy of finding our way back home again. To do that, we need to get very still and quiet. We need to be able to listen to the voice within, calling us Home.

Most of us hustle and rush through our days, forgetting that there even *is* an inner voice whispering an invitation to rest within and enjoy the moment, whatever it may be. Children remind us. They remind us of our natural state — the one buried beneath layers of fear, guardedness, or disengagement from life. They remind us of who we can be if we live with an open heart, in wonder, enchantment, and gratitude. They remind us of the treasures hidden under our own pillow.

Everything we are looking for is here. It is here in our active days, our sleepless nights, the snuggles under Dora the Explorer sheets, and the shouting from the sidelines at baseball games. It is here, the possibility of true expansion of our heart and soul. If we embrace the moment, we will find everything we long for.

There is a glass ceiling that is blessedly being shattered as a generation of parents commit to parenting with greater presence, attunement, and engagement. Doing so is not easy; in fact, for most of us, it is counterintuitive to how we were raised, very much a journey of two steps forward, one step back. But if you make even a small effort to be more awake and engaged with your children, the possibilities are limitless! Not only will you experience greater joy in your heart and peace in your home, but the world will be populated with more and more people who grew up feeling seen, appreciated, and enjoyed. Imagine the magnitude of change *that* will precipitate on this spinning planet of ours!

We have the opportunity to change the world, one child at a time, while healing and transforming ourselves. What an opportunity! What an adventure!

It is indeed a spiritual pilgrimage, raising a child. One precious moment at a time.

Author's Note

Thank you for reading this book. It a blessing and honor to be allowed into your life to share the ideas that have taken form and shape for me over the many years I have taught, counseled, and parented.

If you would like to stay in touch, I hope you'll join our Facebook group at www.facebook.com/SusanStiffelmanAuthor. I engage there regularly with an ever-growing tribe of like-minded, like-hearted parents who are committing to parenting with ever-greater presence.

You may also want to sign up for my newsletter at www.Susan Stiffelman.com or at ParentingWithoutPowerStruggles.com. You can stay current with my activities and appearances, and also access many helpful resources.

If you would like to go deeper with my work, I offer a variety of live and online classes that help transform the ideas I teach into real-life practices. Please visit my website for details. To book me for a speaking event, please contact me at parentingpresence@gmail.com. Finally, if you have a story or insight to share, please write to me at parentingpresence@gmail.com. I take enormous pleasure in hearing how the ideas I write about affect those who read them, and I am always interested in learning from my readers.

With my very best,
Susan Stiffelman

• Acknowledgments •

The writing of this book came at a time of great personal transformation. Long-held limiting beliefs were laid to rest as new possibilities were being birthed, starting with the invitation by Eckhart Tolle and Kim Eng to publish *Parenting with Presence* with New World Library's new imprint, Eckhart Tolle Editions. Not only was I being offered an opportunity to associate with one of the clearest and brightest lights I have ever met, but Eckhart went so far as to help edit the book as I wrote. I cannot adequately express my thanks to both Eckhart and Kim for so deeply believing in my work and championing it so that others may benefit from what I have learned along the way.

To my supercalifragilistic editor, Jason Gardner, thank you, thank you, thank you. There wasn't a moment when I didn't feel comforted by your presence and restored by your good cheer, not to mention your wise edits. To Barbara Moulton, thank you for showing up so wholeheartedly and offering such steady encouragement from the sidelines. And to my wonderful copy editor, Mimi Kusch — what a pleasure it was to work with you.

To those who have participated in my online programs, read my previous book, followed my *Huffpost* column, joined me in teleclasses, or become part of our growing Facebook tribe, you will never know how your emails and comments lift me up and inspire me to continue with my work. At heart, I am something of a layabout. When I think of you — real moms and dads and grandparents and teachers who use and benefit from the ideas I offer — I am motivated to keep on keeping on. Thank you for your encouragement and for letting me know when something has helped.

A special shout-out to Glennon Melton and the Momastery team — Amy Olrick and Amanda Doyle. Your belief in my work and your willingness to offer my classes to your tribe showed me what is possible: that we really can change the world for the better, one child and family at a time. Thank you for leaping with me.

To my mom, for your lightness and love, and for the fact that at ninety-three, you are still opening email attachments and tuning in to my online webinars. Thank you for showing me how great life can be, no matter how old we are. A special thank-you to my extra moms, Beverly Gold and Berenise Kaplan. I love you.

To the most patient, loving, kind, smart, supportive, caring, fun, talented, and incredible man on earth, Paul Stanton — thank you for the miracle of showing up. I thank my lucky stars for you every day, and for our immense and astonishing love. (An extra special thanks for all those delicious meals and foot rubs when I was up against a deadline!)

And finally, to my son, Ari — one of my life's greatest teachers. Thank you for your patience and love as I continue to grow up alongside you. May you be forever blessed.

Notes

Chapter 2. Growing Up While Raising Kids

34 *While the child is having a pain-body attack:* Eckhart Tolle, *A New Earth: Awakening to Your Life's Purpose* (2005; repr., New York: Penguin, 2008), 106.

49 *Imagine yourself drifting along:* This exercise was inspired by John Welwood, *Perfect Love, Imperfect Relationships: Healing the Wound of the Heart* (Boston: Shambhala, 2006).

Chapter 3. Throw Away the Snapshot

53 *In a study published in the journal* Science: Eli Finkel, "The Trauma of Parenthood," *New York Times,* June 29, 2014, www.nytimes.com /2014/06/29/opinion/sunday/the-trauma-of-parenthood.html?_r=0.

73 *Supreme excellence consists of breaking the enemy's resistance:* Sun Tzu, *The Art of War,* trans. Ralph D. Sawyer (New York: Metro Books, 2001), 16.

Chapter 4. We Aren't Raising Children, We're Raising Adults

82 *More teenagers and young adults die from suicide:* D. Shaffer and L. Craft, "Methods of Adolescent Suicide Prevention," *Journal of Clinical Psychiatry* 60, suppl. 2 (1999): 70–74.

83 *Not knowing, in our blood and bones:* John Welwood, *Perfect Love, Imperfect Relationships: Healing the Wound of the Heart* (Boston: Shambhala, 2006), 4.

86 *Self-liking, or an easygoing peace:* Thupten Jinpa, *A Fearless Heart: How the Courage to Be Compassionate Can Transform Our Lives* (New York: Hudson Street Press, 2015).

Chapter 5. Modeling Self-Love and Awareness

91 *The busy lives people lead:* Daniel J. Siegel, *The Mindful Brain: Reflection and Attunement in the Cultivation of Well-Being* (New York: Norton, 2007), 4.

94 *So, your kids must love the iPad?:* Nick Bilton, "Steve Jobs Was a Low-Tech Parent," *New York Times*, September 10, 2104, www.nytimes.com/2014/09/11/fashion/steve-jobs-apple-was-a-low-tech-parent.html?_r=0.

96 *[The problem is that] perpetually doing:* Martha Beck, *The Joy Diet: 10 Daily Practices for a Happier Life* (New York: Crown, 2008), 9.

101 *When one of us was feeling sick:* Bunmi Laditan, "I Miss the Village," *Huffington Post*, July 24, 2014, www.huffingtonpost.com/bunmi-laditan/i-miss-the-village_b_5585677.html.

107 *But people try to silence even that one:* Gavin de Becker, *Protecting the Gift: Keeping Children and Teenagers Safe (and Parents Sane)* (New York: Dell, 1999), 26.

109 *What is the weather like right now:* Eline Snel, *Sitting Still Like a Frog: Mindfulness Exercises for Kids (and Their Parents)* (Boston: Shambhala, 2013), 54.

112 *Wonder without googling:* Janell Burley Hofmann, "Gregory's iPhone Contract," blog, July 8, 2013, www.janellburleyhofmann.com/post journal/gregorys-iphone-contract.

Chapter 8. Cultivating Empathy, Vulnerability, and Compassion

156 *A social impact brand that supports:* Make a Stand website, www.makeastand.com.

158 *Maria Shriver titled:* Maria Shriver, "We're in Need of a Social Kindness Movement," blog, August 17, 2014, mariashriver.com/blog/2014/08/were-in-need-of-a-social-kindness-movement-maria-shriver.

161 *About 15 to 20 percent are on the impulsive end:* Elaine Aron, *The Highly Sensitive Child: Helping Our Children Thrive When the World Overwhelms Them* (New York: Harmony, 2002), 5.

Chapter 9. Helping Our Kids Cope with Stress

165 *10 percent of high school sophomores:* Vicki Abeles, "Crossing the Line: How the Academic Rat Race Is Making Our Kids Sick," *Huffington Post*,

May 19, 2014, www.huffingtonpost.com/vicki-abeles/education-stress _b_5341256.html.

166 *In a study titled "Stress in America":* "Stress in America," American Psychological Association, 2013, www.apa.org/news/press/releases /stress/.

166 *The American Academy of Pediatrics released a study:* Jack P. Shonkoff and Andrew S. Garner, "The Lifelong Effects of Early Childhood Adversity and Toxic Stress," *Pediatrics* (Dec. 26, 2011), Pediatrics.aappublications .org/content/early/2011/12/21/peds.2011-2663.abstract.

167 *People today are more connected to one another:* Michael Price, "Alone in the Crowd: Sherry Turkle Says Social Networking Is Eroding Our Ability to Live Comfortably Offline," *American Psychological Association* 42, no. 6 (June 2011): 26, www.apa.org/monitor/2011/06/social-net working.aspx.

168 *The last time my mother got angry with me:* Arianna Huffington, *Thrive: Third Metric to Redefining Success and Creating a Life of Well-Being, Wisdom, and Wonder* (New York: Harmony, 2104), 8.

169 *Author Johann Hari cites research:* Johann Hari, "The Likely Cause of Addiction Has Been Discovered, and It Is Not What You Think," *Huffington Post*, January 20, 2015, http://www.huffingtonpost.com /johann-hari/the-real-cause-of-addicti_b_6506936.html. Hari is the author of *Chasing the Scream: The First and Last Days of the War on Drugs*.

175 *Mindful seems to imply that the mind is full:* Eckhart Tolle, "Wisdom 2.0," presentation, San Francisco, February 15, 2014, www.youtube.com /watch?v=foU1qgOdtwg.

176 *Because all of those steps we take:* "From the Inside Out: Helping Teachers and Students Nurture Resilience," profile of Linda Lantieri, Mindful .org, www.innerresilience-tidescenter.org/documents/Mindful.Org Oct2014-From_the_Inside_Out_Helping_Teachers_&_Students _Nuture_Resilience.pdf.

178 *My parents were protection, confidence, warmth*: Jacques Lusseyran, *And There Was Light: The Extraordinary Memoir of a Blind Hero of the French Resistance in World War II* (Novato, CA: New World Library, 2014), 2.

186 *This calls to mind a survey:* Sharon Jayson, "Generation Y's Goal? Wealth and Fame," *USA Today*, January 9, 2007, Usatoday30.usatoday .com/news/nation/2007-01-09-gen-y-cover_x.htm.

189 *Epigenetics means 'around the gene':* David Rakel, quoted in "Lifestyle Choices Can Change Your Genes," *UWHealth*, www.uwhealth.org /news/lifestyle-choices-can-change-your-genes/13915.

190 *When NIH researchers measured blood flow:* Kerry J. Ressler and Helen S.

Mayberg, "Targeting Abnormal Neural Circuits in Mood and Anxiety Disorders: From the Laboratory to the Clinic," www.ncbi.nlm.nih.gov /pubmed/17726478.

191 *After years of searching:* Barbara De Angelis, *Secrets about Life Every Woman Should Know: Ten Principles for Total Emotional and Spiritual Fulfillment* (New York: Hyperion, 2000).

Chapter 11. Tools, Tips, and Strategies

208 *I am not the downpour:* Eline Snel, *Sitting Still Like a Frog: Mindfulness Exercises for Kids (and Their Parents)* (Boston: Shambhala, 2013), 55.

214 *Grandparent hugs are mystical:* Bunmi Laditan, *The Honest Toddler: A Child's Guide to Parenting* (New York: Simon and Schuster, 2014), 40.

215 *Feelings are internal and can often be hidden:* Annie Lalla, "What Makes You Cry," *Annie Lalla: Cartographer of Love,* June 10, 2014, Annielalla .com/2014/06/10/makes-cry/.

232 *The more you get your neurons firing:* Rick Hanson, *Take in the Good* newsletter, November 18, 2009, www.rickhanson.net/take-in-the-good.

235 *The typical human mind:* Martha Beck, *The Joy Diet: 10 Daily Practices for a Happier Life* (New York: Crown, 2008), 18.

Additional
• Resources •

Free Resources on My Website

- SusanStiffelman.com/PWPextras: Listen as I guide you through the "Now It's Your Turn" exercises at the end of each chapter.
- Audio clips of Susan coaching parents on a variety of topics.
- Downloadable report on identifying potential causes of power struggles, delivered to newsletter subscribers.
- Love Flooding video, offered to newsletter subscribers.
- And more!

Books

PARTICULARLY VALUABLE FOR PARENTS

Attached at the Heart: Eight Proven Parenting Principles for Raising Connected and Compassionate Children by Barbara Nicholson and Lysa Parker
Brainstorm: The Power and Purpose of the Teenage Brain by Daniel Siegel
The Conscious Parent: Transforming Ourselves, Empowering Our Children by Shefali Tsabary
Conscious Uncoupling by Katherine Woodward Thomas

Emotional Intelligence: Why It Can Matter More Than IQ by Daniel Goleman

Everyday Blessings: The Inner Work of Mindful Parenting by Myla Kabat-Zinn and Jon Kabat-Zinn

Generation Stressed: Play-Based Tools to Help Your Child Overcome Anxiety by Michele Kambolis

Hamlet's Blackberry: Building a God Life in the Digital Age by William Powers

A Handful of Quiet: Happiness in Four Pebbles by Thich Nhat Hanh (a book for young readers)

Hands Free Mama: A Guide to Putting Down the Phone, Burning the To-Do List, and Hold On to Your Kids: Why Parents Need to Matter More Than Peers by Gordon Neufeld

Is Nothing Something?: Kids' Questions and Zen Answers about Life, Death, Family, Friendship, and Everything in Between by Thich Nhat Hanh

Last Child in the Woods: Saving Our Children from Nature-Deficit Disorder by Richard Louv

Letting Go of Perfection to Grasp What Really Matters! by Rachel Macy Stafford

The Mindful Child: How to Help Your Kid Manage Stress and Become Happier, Kinder, and More Compassionate by Susan Kaiser Greenland

Odd Girl Out: The Hidden Culture of Aggression in Girls by Rachel Simmons

Parenting Apart: How Separated and Divorced Parents Can Raise Happy and Secure Kids by Christina McGhee

Playful Parenting by Lawrence J. Cohen

Sitting Still Like a Frog: Mindfulness Exercises for Kids (and Their Parents) by Eline Snel

Teach Like Your Hair's on Fire: The Methods and Madness Inside Room 56 by Rafe Esquith

10 Mindful Minutes: Giving Our Children — and Ourselves — the Social and Emotional Skills to Reduce Stress and Anxiety for Healthier, Happy Lives by Goldie Hawn

GENERALLY WISE AND INSPIRING

Broken Open: How Difficult Times Can Help Us Grow by Elizabeth Lesser

Carry On, Warrior: The Power of Embracing Your Messy, Beautiful Life by Glennon Melton

Daring Greatly: How the Courage to Be Vulnerable Transforms the Way We Live, Love, Parent, and Lead by Brené Brown

Getting the Love You Want: A Guide for Couples by Harville Hendrix
Happy for No Reason: 7 Steps to Being Happy from the Inside Out by Marci
    Shimoff
*I Need Your Love — Is That True?: How to Stop Seeking Love, Approval, and
    Appreciation and Start Finding Them Instead* by Byron Katie
In the Heart of Life: A Memoir by Kathy Eldon
The Joy Diet: 10 Practices for a Happier Life by Martha Beck
*A Mindful Nation: How a Simple Practice Can Help Us Reduce Stress, Improve
    Performance, and Recapture the American Spirit* by Tim Ryan
My Stroke of Insight: A Brain Scientist's Personal Journey by Jill Bolte Taylor
Perfect Love, Imperfect Relationships: Healing the Wound of the Heart by John
    Welwood
*Thrive: The Third Metric to Redefining Success and Creating a Life of Well-
    Being, Wisdom, and Wonder* by Arianna Huffington
Traveling Mercies: Some Thoughts on Faith by Anne Lamott
*Uncovering Happiness: Overcoming Depression with Mindfulness and Self-
    Compassion* by Elisha Goldstein
The War of Art: Break Through the Blocks and Win Your Inner Creative Battles
    by Steven Pressfield
When Things Fall Apart: Heart Advice for Difficult Times by Pema Chödrön

Other Resources and Links

- AttachmentParenting.org: Information on practices pro-
  moting strong emotional bonds between parents and
  their children.
- EckhartTolle.com: Eckhart Tolle's teachings are invaluable for those wanting to live with greater presence.
- GreatHall.com: Award-winning audio recordings that
  make history, mythology, and literary classics come alive
  for children.
- ImpactSelfDefense.org: Impact training is an excellent
  self-defense program.
- LettersToOurFormerSelves.com: Beautiful letters from

people at earlier times in their life, hosted by my son, Ari Andersen.

- MindfulnessCDs.com: Jon Kabat-Zinn has wonderful meditations and programs for mindfulness.
- MindfulSchools.org: Online and live training programs to bring mindfulness into schools.
- RootsOfEmpathy.org: A classroom program focusing on increasing empathy and reducing aggressive behavior.
- TogetherRising.org: An online crowd-sourced program providing needed support to women who in turn uplift their families and communities.
- VolunteerMatch.org: An easy way to find age and interest-appropriate volunteer opportunities.
- TheWork.com: I love the work of Byron Katie and the way it helps dissipate the effects of stressful thoughts.

Index

About the Author

Photo: Paul Stanton

S usan Stiffelman is the author of *Parenting Without Power Struggles: Raising Joyful, Resilient Kids While Staying Cool, Calm, and Connected* and is the *Huffington Post*'s weekly "Parent Coach" advice columnist. She is a licensed marriage and family therapist, a credentialed teacher, and an international speaker. Susan is also an aspiring banjo·player, a middling but determined tap-dancer, and an optimistic gardener.

ParentingPresence@gmail.com
www.SusanStiffelman.com

About Eckhart Tolle Editions

Eckhart Tolle Editions was launched in 2015 to publish life-changing works, both old and new, that have been personally selected by Eckhart Tolle. This imprint of New World Library presents books that can powerfully aid in transforming consciousness and awakening readers to a life of purpose and presence.

Learn more about Eckhart Tolle at

www.eckharttolle.com